all about
discus . . .
by
Dr. Herbert R. Axelrod

with supplements by
**Dr. Leonard P. Schultz
Guenther Keller
Dr. Gottfried Schubert
Dr. Robert J. Goldstein
Jack Wattley
Dr. Robert W. Burke**

© 1970 by T.F.H. Publications
Revised edition. © 1972 by T.F.H. Publications, Inc., Ltd.
Revised edition. © 1978 by T.F.H. Publications, Inc., Ltd.

ISBN 0-87666-035-9

Distributed in the U.S. by T.F.H. Publications, Inc., 211 West Sylvania Avenue, PO Box 427, Neptune, NJ 07753; in England by T.F.H. (Gt. Britain) Ltd., 13 Nutley Lane, Reigate, Surrey; in Canada to the pet trade by Rolf C. Hagen Ltd., 3225 Sartelon Street, Montreal 382, Quebec; in Southeast Asia by Y.W. Ong, 9 Lorong 36 Geylang, Singapore 14; in Australia and the South Pacific by Pet Imports Pty. Ltd., P.O. Box 149, Brookvale 2100, N.S.W. Australia; in South Africa by Valid Agencies, P.O. Box 51901, Randburg 2125 South Africa. Published by T.F.H. Publications, Inc., Ltd, the British Crown Colony of Hong Kong.

It is very difficult, or even impossible to identify which species a particular discus may belong to without a clear side view photograph. For the non-ichthyologist the identification is made primarily on the basis of the vertical bars and the horizontal streak patterns. Photo by Gerhard Budich.

Contents

Three pioneers in the breeding of discusfishes from all over the world. Top left, Danny DiCoco lives in New Jersey and is a house painter by profession. He has bred all species of discus except the Lake Tefe *Symphysodon aequifasciata aequifasciata*. He has also successfully hybridized the other discusfishes in all combinations. He supplied the New York market with tank-bred discus for many years from about 1956 to 1966. Dr. Eduard Schmidt-Focke, also known as Dr. Eduard Schmidt, is a gynecologist practicing medicine in Bad Homburg, Germany. He has been a life-long breeder of fishes and loves discus more than any. He has successfully bred all the species of discus and is probably the only man in the world to have done so since only Harald Schultz and Dr. Herbert R. Axelrod ever brought back the true Lake Tefe green discus *Symphysodon aequifasciata aequifasciata* which has a green body and dark brown stripes. He has successfully hybridized all species of discus. The lower photo shows the manager of Chao Phraya Aquarium, Bangkok, Thailand who has been successfully breeding discus, especially the "true, blue" discus, *Symphyosodon discus*, and supplying breeding stock to most of southeast Asia. His name is Virachai. Photos by Dr. Herbert R. Axelrod.

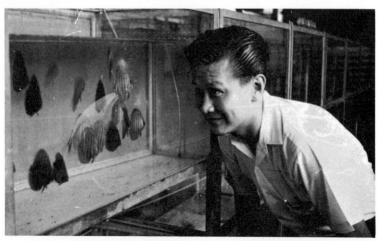

FOREWORD

The discus has for many years been considered among dedicated hobbyists as *the* fish. To many of them, it is king of aquarium fishes; to all, it is a challenge.

With the possible exception of Mr. W. T. Dodd, who in 1949 was the first person to breed discus in quantity, and Mr. Jack Wattley, who lays claim to secret knowledge on rearing fry without parental aid, I do not know anyone (among the many who have tried) who has found it profitable as a vocation to breed discus. There are no commercial hatcheries except in Hong Kong, Singapore, and perhaps in Bangkok, where breeding discus is a specialty. And I know of no hatchery owner in the world whose sole source of income is from tank-bred discus (whereas I know many who breed nothing but angelfish, danios, or neons).

Who tries to breed the discus commercially? Fish fanciers, whether beginners or long-established professionals, are almost invariably tempted sooner or later, by the premium prices commanded on the market, to attempt propagating the fish. Most of them soon discover that more dollars are going out than are coming in and that discus breeding is not a money-making occupation.

Please do not misunderstand what I am trying to convey. Hundreds of persons have been successful in breeding discus and a few have been intermittently fortunate enough to realize a profit in avocational breeding ventures. Most of those whose success has become well-known, such as Dr. Eduard Schmidt, a medical practitioner in Frankfurt, Germany; Danny DiCocco of New Jersey, who lives in a house that fish built; and a group at Chao Phraya Aquarium in Bangkok, were or are hobbyists primarily. All of them had a few pairs of breeding discus and met with much more than customary success yet all of them repeatedly disposed of their stock in complete frustration over varied factors that caused failures. None of them, despite renewed endeavors, has discovered how to induce spawning with sufficient frequency or regularity and to rear the fry consistently enough to earn a living as discus breeders.

Though I have been a discus enthusiast for many years I was not trying to breed them. My interest focused on studying them in the wild and collecting them, hopefully to learn enough of their lives in their Brazilian habitat and as aquarium dwellers so that I could breed them in the future. After eighteen years of collecting discus in Brazil, I have learned how to catch them in large numbers but have discovered nothing that would help me in breeding them except the characteristics of water and ecology they prefer and the foods that they eat. Observations of discus in captivity have revealed what substitute foods are satisfactory and what simulations of natural environment are acceptable.

In this book I will discuss what I and other experts have learned about the various discus fishes. I can tell how they taste, for I have eaten hundreds of them on collecting trips; where they are to be found and how they are collected will be discussed, and included will be information on how to identify them and the color varieties in which they occur. Supplementing this will be reports from various hobbyists regarding their experiences and observations in maintaining and breeding discus. But there will not be anything herein about making money breeding discus— except that you should not expect to.

Geronico photo of Harald Schultz and Coboclos eating blue discus.

1. THE DISCUS AT HOME

The discus is chiefly a Brazilian fish though some adjacent areas in eastern Colombia and Peru, and possibly even Venezuela, may harbor a limited number of them. I have found that *every* river system in proximity to the Amazon, from the Lake Tefé region inhabited by the green discus through the thousands of miles to the home of the brown discus near Belem do Para at the mouth of the Amazon, contains huge colonies of discus in nearly every suitable environment.

I have collected discus all along the Amazon, but never actually in this mighty river. Most of the Amazon is fast-flowing and very muddy, and discus are not found in turbulent or silted waters. They frequent placid water and show a preference for lakes and such intermittent rivers as are so depleted in flow during dry seasons that strings of lakes are formed. Such is the Urubu River near Itacoatiara, Brazil. With the assistance of commercial food-fishermen, I have caught thousands of discus in some of the lakes in this locality.

Wild discus are not to be found in water that is alkaline; they inhabit waters of varying degree of acidity, usually very soft, never crystal clear, and never deep. They are seldom seen in open water and prefer to remain close to a sunken log, a rock, or a fallen tree. Some collectors assert that discus are *always* found in habitats frequented by *Pterophyllum* and *Cichlasoma festivum*, but such has not been my observation. I know from experience that *C. festivum* may inhabit polluted water that discus would never tolerate.

Anyone in search of discus should explore rivers relatively close to the Amazon. If the search is extended more than a few hundred

7

miles distant, especially southward, there is little likelihood of success. But in less remote, large, slow-flowing rivers there will be discus. A huge tree which has fallen into such a river because of bank erosion should be sought. A night visit by dugout will probably be productive. A strong light will afford visibility to a depth of several feet into quiet water, and poking with a stick among underwater branches of the fallen tree will in all probability reveal the presence of discusfish, especially in the dry season.

Slow-flowing water of a typical discus habitat, with roots and fallen branches providing refuges. Dr. Herbert R. Axelrod photo.

This native fish is well known to most Brazilians, whether Coboclos or Indians. It is known both in the vernacular Portuguese and in the *lingua geral* of the aborigines as *acara discu*. Though the discusfish is difficult to catch and is too bony to be a choice food fish, it is a staple item of diet among most of the inhabitants of the Amazon Basin. It is the practice among Indians of Brazil to poison the water of small lakes and leisurely moving streams with *timbo* (raw rotenone) root by beating the fleshy root into a pulp and allowing the extruded sap to diffuse through the water. Both the dead and the near-dead victims of the poison soon rise to the surface and are gathered into the nets of the fishermen. There are almost always a few discus in the catch, and these too are eaten. They have the flavor of flounder when fried.

I must admit that in my enthusiasm on collecting trips I sometimes caught more discus than I should have and in such circumstances always lost many of them through overcrowding in the halved 55-gallon gasoline drums used as holding tanks. But those that suffocated in this manner were eaten, and losses among

Brazilians checking a likely area for finding a congregation of discus. Dr. Herbert R. Axelrod photo.

the survivors were reduced in that I was not required to stop for collection of other food and could more speedily reach civilization and facilities for providing the fishes better care. It is doubtful that even half of the discus collected in Brazil ever reach a foreign shore, and many of those surviving transportation from the jungle die before becoming acclimated to life in captivity.

Collecting discus is not easy; they are usually caught one by one. Very young discus are rarely captured, because they hide among branches of fallen trees and are difficult to see and more difficult to net from their tangled refuge. Larger discus can be caught at

Natives placing net to entrap discus in their sanctuary beneath a fallen branch.

night by blinding them with a strong light and snaring them with a dip net before they dart away. I have also found it expedient to pass a large seine completely around a fallen tree to trap the fish within the enclosure. With the help of a group of Indians, the tree is then chopped into sections small enough for removal and the trapped discus can be captured. There are two objections to wide-spread use of this method. First of all, the particular environment attractive to these fish is destroyed; secondly, if most of the discus in the locality are at hand when the seine is placed, few of the species are left for repopulation of that area.

The smaller discus available from dealers are usually tank-bred, either locally propagated or imported from the Orient. Regardless of the hobbyist's objective, it is more advisable to buy a half dozen small discus than to invest the same amount of money in purchasing a pair of larger ones. The smaller ones are usually stronger and likely to be less heavily infested by parasites. Freshly captured discus are seldom entirely free of parasites, and they usually encounter others while being held for acclimatization and awaiting arrangements for export. Unfortunately there are no sophisticated exporters in Amazonian Brazil, and it is doubtful that the market would support one. By the time a large specimen reaches the local market, it will almost always die within a year from the ravages of disease or internal parasites.

A sixty-foot nylon seine being placed to deny access to refuges along the banks; after discus are forced into midstream, they are caught by using a casting net. Harald Schultz photos.

Various procedures preparatory to collecting fishes overcome with the poisonous juice of the rotenone-bearing root; subsequently the fishes rise to the surface and are gathered. Harald Schultz photos.

2. DISTINCTIONS AMONG DISCUS

For many years discus have been confusingly identified. The genesis of mis-identification undoubtedly lies with the publication by Dr. William T. Innes of photographs of two species as representatives of *Symphysodon discus* Heckel 1840. A good many years after Innes' publication appeared, I went to Brazil and made extensive collections of discus which enabled Dr. Leonard P. Schultz, then Curator of Fishes of the Smithsonian Institute, to re-evaluate the whole genus. Since Dr. Schultz reclassified these fishes there has been a considerable amount of criticism from persons relatively uninformed on the subject. The primary evidence for this criticism is neither taxonomic data nor field evidence; disputation is founded solely from the fact that it is possible to crossbreed captive discus designated as belonging to different species and/or subspecies.

I am inclined to remind these amateur "ichthyologists" (and none of the critics I have in mind has earned an advanced degree in the study of taxonomy, the classification of living organisms) that a large number of fishes can be crossed when separated from their kind in an aquarium but that this does not necessarily indicate that they will interbreed in nature. In most cases I would be suspicious of a so-called species if I discovered the existence of populations in nature which exhibited characteristics suggesting that supposedly different species had interbred in some area where their ranges overlapped.

Although the possibility of interbreeding and producing fertile offspring is a factor to be considered in determining separate specific classification, just to succeed in crossing two species in an aquarium does not of itself invalidate designation of these two

When Innes published this photo in 1934 of a discus spawning, everyone, including Innes, thought the colorful fish to be a male in spawning coloration, when in fact two species were involved in the spawning. This "male" is *Symphysodon aequifasciata aequifasciatia*, the first "turquoise" discus. Photo by William T. Innes.

fishes as distinct species. Those who are inclined toward making judgments on such slim evidence might well be referred to the works of the late Dr. Myron Gordon wherein he discussed the relative ease with which various species of *Xiphophorus* can be freely interbred in captivity while seldom, if ever, breeding interspecifically in nature, even though the fishes often occupy the same bodies of water. In his book *Rivulins of the Old World* and in other writings of Col. Jorgen Scheel of Denmark, there are accounts of scores of crosses made in aquariums between various species of killifishes, especially among species of the genus *Aphyosemion*. Doubtless other reports of interspecific crosses could be gleaned from scientific literature, especially concerning such ordinarily easy-to-spawn fishes as most cichlids and some trouts and carps.

How then do we account for such fish as may be called *real blue discus, royal blue discus*, or *Wattley's turquoise discus*, the like of which make an occasional appearance in almost every population of discus fishes? I have carefully studied thousands of discus, both those I have collected in the wild and those which have been tank-bred, and the occurrence of an intensely colored discus in random spawnings is a rarity in either environment.

I have theorized about these exceptionally colored fishes. In many tank communities, as among swordtails, platies, and mollies, and among the more complex *Aphyosemion* species of Africa, exceptional individuals are often found. Whether they are more intensely colored or have longer finnage than most of their kind, these individuals are almost always males. Such a fish may be analogous to the occasional person who grows seven feet tall. While I have not researched the point extensively, my conversations with several scientists indicate that these exceptionally developed human beings are also usually male.

Therefore, my inclination is to call these exceptional fishes "dominant males." If such a fish is mated with his mother or with his sisters, it is possible in many cases to develop a strain through a considerable amount of further selective breeding so that the characteristics of the extraordinary individuals are fixed as characters of the strain. Nearly all of our "fancy" varieties of domestic animals, dogs, cats, chickens, and the like have been developed through similar inbreeding techniques from just such "dominant male" ancestors—or "sports," as they are called by geneticists.

Such sports, or mutants, occur in nature, and I have seen these extraordinarily colorful individuals, particularly among tetras, that stood out in a school of perhaps several thousand fish. In random matings within a multitudinous school, pairing of the exceptional male with his mother or a sister would be very unlikely indeed, and further close inbreeding would be astronomically remote in probability unless some particular influence were in operation. If my theory is extended to endow the unique individual with additional characteristics which enable him to play a sort of limited "bull of the herd" role within the school, he might attract a certain following and perhaps also function with more females than a normal male and thus enhance the probability of mating with such close relatives in sufficient number to cause his genetic strain to become somewhat established. In future random matings, when two of the fish that have inherited from him the gene or genes producing the trait chance to pair, and during the involved processes of meiosis there eventually occurs the exact coupling or crossover of genes required, another "dominant male" will appear among the fry.

Dr. Eduard Schmidt photo of *Symphysodon aequifasciata haraldi* and fry.

In nature these "dominant males" are found rarely and singly among normally developed fish, and my theory would account for the occasional incidence of such distinctly different individuals. The market-named "blue" discus strains are sports also, not distinct species, and their production in numbers is brought about only through the manipulations of breeders. No one has ever bred a pair of such "blues" and produced a first generation of offspring in which all or most of the fry, or even a majority of one sex, were as colorful as either of the parents. Thus we are not considering a species. On the other hand, the fishes we know as brown discus, green discus, and blue discus occur as populations in the wild, and a mating of any two fish from one of these designated groups produces fry that are replicas of the parents, so it is beyond my understanding to fathom the reasoning of critics who would class these fishes as intergradients and not entitled to specific or sub-specific classification.

3. DISCUS DIET

In earlier days, fanciers fed their discus exclusively upon live foods, principally tubifex worms, white worms, and daphnia. Dietary supplements included brine shrimp, mosquito larvae, and wingless strains of the fruit fly. Some aquarists also propagated guppies and added their fry to the discus menu.

Live foods are still being fed, but animals captured afield present a hazard in that they often carry disease or parasitic organisms which are dangerous to fishes. Live tubifex are extremely dangerous in this respect. Fortunately some of these food animals are now marketed after being put through a freeze-drying process during which they are sterilized. Among these freeze-dried foods are tubifex worms, fairy shrimp, brine shrimp, mosquito larvae, and daphnia; liver and beef are also offered in this form by dealers, and both are excellent for feeding discus.

The above-mentioned freeze-dried brine shrimp should not be confused with frozen brine shrimp. Almost all of the frozen brine shrimp now available are more than 90% water; water of course, has no nutritive value, and most of it must be squeezed from the shrimp meat before feeding or a fouling of the aquarium will result. A caution too about brine shrimp eggs: it is advisable to check the packaging label or inquire as to their source, as eggs from certain localities contain concentrations of DDT which may be dangerous. Until the ecological situation of such areas is cleared up or a method is discovered for treatment of DDT-contaminated eggs to make them usable, they should be regarded with suspicion. And since the use of this insecticide is widespread, it may well be that live foods collected anywhere, unless from locations remote from agricultural areas, would be unfit for feeding fishes.

The flake foods are nutritional supplements to the discus diet, but *the* food discus seem to thrive on is white worms (*Enchytraeus albidus*). These are not presently available in freeze-dried form, but they are not difficult to culture, and living worms may be ordered through dealers. Suitable for white worm culture is a wooden, plastic, or enamelware container with a close-fitting glass or metal cover to retain moisture in the equal-parts fill mixture of humus and peat moss. (An occasional sprinkling with water may also be required.) Just before introducing the starter stock of worms, a thin layer of cooked oatmeal and condensed milk or milk-soaked bread is put in and lightly covered. This will be eaten in three or four days and must be continually replenished. Best results are obtained at a temperature of about 55°; at 35° there is no breeding, and above 75° the worms die. After about six weeks, harvesting of the worms may begin; they will usually be found clinging in clusters to the walls of the container and may be easily removed for feeding to the fishes.

White worm size may be compared with paper match in the G. J. M. Timmerman photo; Robert Gannon pictures the removal of a squirming cluster with scissors.

A one-food diet isn't any more nearly adequate for the discus than for the discus-keeper, and a variety is mandatory to maintain discus in healthful condition. Feedings should be made at least twice daily, but it is better practice to feed smaller portions at more frequent intervals. The proper amount of food to dispense at a feeding must be learned by observation until apportionment is not in excess of what will be eaten within five minutes. All food that is not eaten should be removed immediately.

Whether or not uneaten food is involved, the accumulation of detritus should be prevented by siphoning as much as possible from the bottom, effecting a change of five to ten per cent of the water daily or at least several times weekly. This will necessitate making provisions for storing and conditioning a considerable amount of water, but frequent partial replacements of water in tanks housing discus is almost as important to their health as proper feeding. Tap water heated to the proper temperature is usually acceptable if not more than 10% is changed daily.

A sparsely furnished breeding tank photographed by Dr. Herbert R. Axelrod and the set-up of photo-contest winner Alex DeZutter, which is attractive though discus are too susceptible to disease to thrive in a community aquarium.

4. HOUSING FOR DISCUS

When man removes an animal from its native habitat and subjects it to life in a different environment the captive is faced with a traumatic situation. A wild creature experiences shock in being captured; if it survives this shock and the possible injuries sustained during capture and the handling and conditions to which it is subjected before reaching a fancier, it must yet become acclimated to the environment then provided. The least that should be done is to furnish suitable substitute foods and to provide housing that approximates as closely as possible the natural environment of the captive.

Most important in the successful keeping of any fish is the temperature and quality of the water, and discus are in some respects more demanding than most fishes regarding water quality. Clear, clean water in a clean aquarium is a must, and periodic partial changes are imperative. Soft water (2 or 3 DH) about pH 6.5–6.8 at approximately 76° temperature and 18 to 24 inches deep is most suitable.

Discus are not ordinary fish. Even in their native Brazilian haunts they are very seldom found in mixed company. Their well-being is not at all enhanced by the presence of tankmates of other genera, especially if the ultimate intention is to breed them. Though I have seen discus spawnings in tanks containing *Corydoras* catfishes, the meticulous "housecleaning" necessary for maintaining discus in optimum condition precludes the need for scavengers.

Mature discus are large fish and require roomy quarters. Presuming that breeding is intended, and in the knowledge that discus, like most other cichlids, prefer to choose their own mates, the best practice is to establish a breeding stock by purchasing a number of young fish and letting them pair off.

Choosing five young fish from a tank that contained roughly equal proportions of males and females would almost guarantee the possession of at least one pair. Assuming about two inches maximum vertical measurement for these five fish, a 20-gallon aquarium would be the smallest practical housing facility; where discus are concerned, the bigger the better.

Once pairings are made, each couple should, if possible, be placed alone in an aquarium that will be their permanent abode. The trauma of capture and the possibility of injury is present on every occasion that a fish is netted; unnecessary moving of all fishes, particularly discus, should be avoided. Such disturbances sometimes instigate "hunger strikes," even to the point of starvation, or death stemming from organic attack aggravated by debility.

In a discus aquarium intended only for display, an arrangement of stones on a shallow bed of gravel can be attractive and may serve to provide the fish a feeling of security. If further decoration is desired, plastic plants or one or two potted plants are suggested. Artificial plants are preferable in several respects: they are more easily kept free of algae and settlings of falling food and debris; there are none of the problems encountered with diseased or normally deteriorating tissues of living plants, and they do not require light.

If the aquarium is to be set up for breeding, a minimum of clutter is desirable and discussion will follow in the chapter on breeding. But first, a word about aquariums in general. Poisons, disease organisms, and parasites are scourges, any one of which can negate all efforts and plans. Never put an aquarium into use or reuse without first cleaning and sterilizing it. Never introduce an unsterilized plant or object into the aquarium, and never put in a fish until it has been isolated in quarantine for at least a week or two and you feel assured that it is free of disease and parasites. Any pet shop specializing in aquarium products can supply the necessary disinfectants and sterilizers.

5. BREEDING DISCUS

The only essential, besides water, in a breeding tank is a solid substrate upon which the eggs are to be deposited, and it might reasonably be argued that the floor or sides of the tank would serve if no other spawning site were available. Some breeders insist that a potted Amazon swordplant provides the best surface, being a natural setting, and I have seen discus eggs deposited on stems or leaves of various plants—and also on the pots that held them, and on plastic plants. All of the discus eggs I have seen in nature, however, were placed upon smooth surfaces of submerged branches which had become denuded of bark, but a wood surface is difficult to keep clean and sterile and is thus usually unsatisfactory for aquarium use. Most breeders prefer ceramic pottery or relatively smooth stones such as slate or the black volcanic glass called obsidian. The familiar reddish-orange flower pot is commonly used, and several breeders attribute their success to usage of orange-colored materials whether or not of ceramic nature.

Although filtration and aeration are not essential in a very large tank at least not until the fry are hatched, it is advisable to provide both. Filtration solves most of the problems of keeping the water as clear as the discus prefer it, and the movement of water effected by aeration is beneficial in several respects. An outside filter is better than an ordinary inside type because it occupies no tank space, but either must be provided with a strip of cheesecloth or other screening device over the intake opening or fry may be sucked into the filter. An undergravel filter is best, and no precautions are necessary regarding fry.

Maintaining water temperature was accomplished by early-day aquarists by applying heat to the tank bottom. More modern methods are to use individual aquarium heaters or to place the tanks in a room with thermostatically controlled heat. The latter is the superior system in that water and surrounding air are kept at nearly the same temperature, but home facilities may not be adaptable to such a set-up, and equipping a breeding room with special heating might involve more expense than could be justified for a small number of tanks.

Whether or not it is significant, I have never seen a productive discus breeding set-up employing a vertical heater. All successful discus breeders of my acquaintance either use a thermostatically controlled submergible type such as the Jäger heater or heat the aquarium room. Though discus may spawn at the 76° temperature regularly maintained, a daily rise of 1° for about four or five days has been found to be extremely effective in conditioning them to spawn. And finally, regarding water, it has been my observation that discus do not spawn in water shallower than 12 inches or deeper than 24 inches.

Providing privacy for spawning discus is placed at high premium by all breeders. To insure maximum privacy, many of them completely cover each tank with paper as soon as spawning occurs. It is certain that discus are reluctant to spawn under conditions of disturbance, whether by persons coming to witness

Discus guarding and fanning eggs deposited on a sturdy leaf blade. Gunter Senfft photo.

S. aequifasciata axelrodi
In Gerhard Budich's spawning sequence photos, the first shows the fry as newly free-swimming.

the proceedings or by the aquarist poking about, and startled fish may devour their spawn. They usually become accustomed to the regularity of feedings and to the cleaning and siphoning, followed by the stimulating addition of fresh water, and they are not upset by these in-schedule events.

For many years discus confounded prospective breeders. Many of them were successful in providing inducements to spawn, but the fry refused to eat and soon died. Their cardinal mistake was being too protective. Knowing that cichlids are likely to eat their eggs or fry in certain circumstances, breeders removed the parents after spawning was completed. Eventually the mystery was solved—the fry subsisted during an early period of life upon exudations from the skin of their parents and did not survive without it. (Subsequent discoveries reveal that the fry of certain other cichlids, such as the orange chromide, *Etroplus maculatus*, subsist to a lesser extent upon parental secretions but are not as dependent upon it as are discus.)

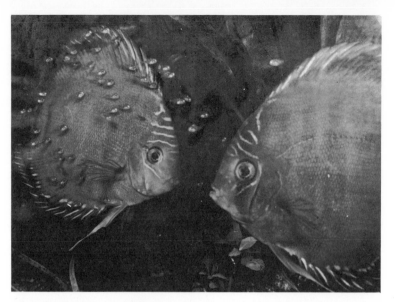

S. aequifasciata axelrodi

Upon hatching, discus fry hang for a time at the spawning site, or elsewhere if the parents choose to move them, and subsist upon their yolk-sacs during this period. After a few days they become free-swimming and then feed upon the mucus covering the bodies of their parents. Perhaps in another week, but more usually about ten or twelve days later, the fry are able to feed upon newly-hatched brine shrimp. Extended bellies of reddish color will be observed if brine shrimp nauplii are being ingested. With evidence of two or three successive feedings, the breeder may safely separate fry and parents. (If the young die, they were probably poisoned by DDT in the brine shrimp.)

The "secret method" of rearing fry apart from their parents is not secret as to method, only in regard to the ingredients of the nutrient solution provided as a dietary substitute for parental slime. The fry are placed in shallow pans with the water depth at about two inches so that the food solution is not too much dispersed for the fry to find it, and to facilitate maintenance of the clean water that is essential. Agar-agar or a similar base rich in proteins is used by several breeders; unrevealed as yet is what vitamins and other additives are used to compound an adequate food.

During their first days the fry feed upon skin secretions of both parents, generally upon one at a time, and a shake of the body (just given in the opposite photo) is the signal to transfer attentions to the other parent. Gerhard Budich photos.

6. DISEASES OF DISCUS

If discus were as easily maintained and bred as guppies, mollies, and platies, chances are that discus fanciers would not be interested in keeping them. Most discus fanciers are persons who desire what is rare or distinctive. To indulge this desire, they must pay the price, since discus are "problem fish" regardless of what anyone may say to the contrary. They are, in fact, more difficult to maintain than a common marine aquarium, and a discouraged discus-keeper might be heartened to find keeping coral reef fishes easier. But challenge adds zest to the endeavor, and a tank of mature discus makes a magnificent display.

Discus are accused of going on "hunger strikes," which smacks of anthropomorphism in relating the fasting of a fish to the actions of a spoiled child who sulks for some trivial reason. Stubborn deportment is founded in reasoning and attempting to gain an end by reprehensible behavior. Fishes are not capable of such subterfuge, and it has been suggested that refusing to eat has a purely physical cause—in regard to the health of the fish or in a property of the environment.

An ailing fish may suffer loss of appetite in the course of development of the ailment. A seemingly unimportant event may put a fish "off its feed" if it is sickly, or some unknown factor associated with the event may be serious enough to affect a healthy fish. In either circumstance, failing to take nourishment aggravates the situation and the fish continues to decline physically until death occurs, or it recovers from its illness or becomes acclimatized to the upsetting factor and regains its appetite.

Discus are extremely susceptible to disease, another reason why they are not suited to life in a community aquarium, and they are almost certain to be afflicted by any ailment suffered by tank-mates. Since they are timid and will likely be harassed or startled to some extent by more active fishes in the community, they exist in an atmosphere of tension and are therefore less resistant to contagion and the ravages of internal parasites. Most aquarists who have maintained community aquariums for some time have had the puzzling experience of losing every barb, molly, platy, and swordtail from an outbreak of disease such as ich, tailrot, or mouth fungus which left tetras seemingly unaffected, and then losing the tetras (which are very sensitive to most dyes) when malachite green, or even a drug containing methylene blue, was used in an effort to rid the tank of the attacking organism.

Discus do not die precipitously when afflicted, as do many smaller fishes, and disease or parasitic infestation may be far progressed before the aquarist becomes aware of the situation. Then the fish are often killed, not by the ailment but by the chemicals added to their water in efforts to effect a cure. Those fishes which have a considerable amount of fat in the body tissues store therein substances which are in excess of current needs and build up (bio-magnification) a reserve for future use. Such poisons and some heavy metals, even when available in almost undetectable quantities, are also stored in this manner because organs of the fish are unable to break them down into chemical forms that can be metabolized or excreted.

The effects of such bio-magnification are usually undetected until catastrophe strikes. Realization that something is amiss generally comes only when the fish stop eating. While the aquarist searches for a solution to the problem, the discus subsist upon the stored materials within the fatty tissues and are killed as these poisons are released into their systems.

Studies of imported discus reveal that most of them carry internal parasites capable of causing death. Thus far no one has marketed a medicine effective in controlling these invaders. For the commercial line of Miracle drugs, with which I am personally involved, a control for intestinal parasites is in the experimental stage, but marketing problems are difficult to overcome. Making sales is not the obstacle; a reputable distributor aims to market a product that will be entirely satisfying to the purchaser. Most hobbyists do not know when their fishes have internal parasites and when they do, many of them would fail to administer accurate dosages. Treatments are usually specified by dosage of a given amount of the medicinal preparation per gallon of water, and until a drug can be developed which is both potent enough to be efficacious and reasonably harmless when too liberally administered, one hesitates to offer it to the public.

The potency required of a drug to be effective against tenacious parasites is such that dosage must be meticulous, and a slight error in dispensation can be disastrous. Few hobbyists know the water content of an aquarium. The true capacity of a tank must be calculated by making allowance for the water displaced by fishes, gravel, plants, accessories, and everything else placed in the tank, and for the unfilled space between the top rail and the waterline. Only by such computation is the actual volume of water determined. A tank rated at fifty gallons and set up in typical fashion probably contains about forty gallons of water; a medicinal dosage measured for fifty gallons would be a 25% overdose and possibly a lethal one.

Imminent death is often indicated among discus by a darkening of color, and a fish may be black at the time it dies.

So far as is currently known, the so-called "discus disease" or "hole-in-the-head disease" afflicts only discus. What are mistaken for worms are actually discharges of pus and other matter which are actuated by water currents to simulate worm-like movements. Additional information on this condition, and upon other points discussed, will be found in the supplementary material that follows.

7. DISCUSsion

Following is discussion by other writers whose work has been submitted to *Tropical Fish Hobbyist* for publication. A certain amount of repetition is inevitable to avoid taking material out of context, and what difference of opinion may be expressed is welcomed.

If everyone shared the same opinions and followed the same procedures, much of the present lore of aquarists would still be shrouded in mystery. Doubters and nonconformists who branch out to test new ways of doing things should report their findings to the hobbyist magazine of their choice so that their information may be shared with others through publication.

A REVIEW OF THE POMPADOUR OR DISCUS FISHES, GENUS *SYMPHYSODON* OF SOUTH AMERICA.

BY DR. LEONARD P. SCHULTZ
United States National Museum
(From the June 1960 issue of *Tropical Fish Hobbyist*)

Nearly three years ago Herbert R. Axelrod informed me that he had specimens of at least four different color varieties of *Symphysodon* and asked if I would like to study them. Naturally, my curiosity was aroused and I wrote him that I would need specimens of each variety, so Mr. Axelrod made a trip to South America to collect specimens with the assistance of Harald Schultz. These specimens were donated to the United States National Museum and form the basis of this paper. Much credit should go to these two men for their great effort in obtaining specimens of the discus fishes.

For several months I have been counting and measuring various characters on specimens of *Symphysodon*. In the meantime, Mr. Axelrod has furnished several excellent color transparencies of the living specimens, that were later preserved and sent to me.

This review of the genus *Symphysodon* leaves certain questions unanswered and it must not be considered the last word on this group. We do not know the extent of the area occupied by each species or subspecies nor do we know the amount of intergradation of the color pattern between the subspecies. It may be possible for aquarists to explore some of these problems and thus advance our knowledge.

The purposes of this paper are to make known to aquarists and to scientists that at least four different kinds of discus, *Symphysodon*, do occur in South America and that a great amount of study is still needed to learn about their life history and ecology.

32

Mature brown discus, *Symphysodon aequifasciata axelrodi*, photographed in Czechoslovakia by Miloslav Kocar. The fish in the background is a veil angelfish, *Pterophyllum* species.

GENUS *SYMPHYSODON*

Symphysodon Heckel, Ann. Wiener Mus., vol. 2, p. 332, 1840 (type species, *Symphysodon discus* Heckel); Eigenmann and Bray, Ann. New York Acad. Sci., vol. 7, p. 623, 1894 (Revision); Regan, Ann. Mag. Nat. Hist. ser. 7, vol. 16, p. 440, 1905 (Revision).

Characters in common for all species: A single pair of nasal openings; ctenoid scales rather small, from 44 to 61 vertical rows from rear edge of head to base of caudal fin rays; scales occur about halfway to tips of dorsal and anal fins; basal third of caudal rays scaled; pectoral and pelvic fins naked; cheek below eye scaled; opercle, subopercle and interopercle scaled; gill rakers absent on upper part of first gill arch with about five short ones on lower part of arch; lips thick and fleshy; teeth small, conical, in a single row; branchiostegal membranes joined across isthmus and free from it; nine vertical dark bars on head and body.

Dorsal rays: IX or X, 30 to 33; anal: VII to IX, 26 to 33; pectoral rays: ii, 7 to 9, iii or iv; pelvic rays: I, 5; branched caudal rays: usually 7 + 7, sometimes 7 + 6.

KEY TO THE SPECIES OF *SYMPHYSODON*

1a. Vertical scale rows about 44 to 48 from rear of head in a straight line to midbase of caudal fin rays; three of the nine vertical dark bars, numbers one, five and nine notably much darker than the others; background coloration of alternating blue and reddish-brown lengthwise streaks; eye blue; no patch of isolated scales behind eye.

discus Heckel

1b. Vertical scale rows 50 to 61; all of the vertical dark bars of approximate intensity except first and last may be a little darker, but the middle or fifth bar not darker than adjoining bars.
3a. Lengthwise streaks dark brown on a dark green background; eye reddish brown.

aequifasciata aequifasciata Pellegrin

3b. Lengthwise streaks bright blue on a light brown background; eye bright red.

aequifasciata haraldi, new subspecies

2b. No lengthwise streaks present on body or fins, although a few blue streaks may occur on forehead; vertical dark bars purple on an olive colored background; eye red; no isolated patch of scales opposite dorsoposterior part of eye a little above the upper end of the preopercular groove.

aequifasciata axelrodi, new subspecies

SYMPHYSODON DISCUS HECKEL

Symphysodon discus Heckel, Ann. Wiener Mus., vol. 2, pp. 332–333, pl. 30, figs. 21–24b, 1840 (type locality Rio Negro); Kner, Sitzber. Akad. Wiss. Wien, vol. 46, p. 299, pl. 2, fig. 2, 1862; Steindachner (in part), Sitzber. Akad. Wiss. Wien, vol. 71, p. 46, 1875 (Amazon at Teffé, Rio Xingu at Poroto do Moz; Rio Madeira at Maues; Rio Negro).

Since I have not been able to examine the specimens on which the following references were based, they may refer to species of *Symphysodon* other than *S. discus* Heckel: Günther, Catalog of the Fishes in the British Museum, vol. 4, p. 316, 1862 (Rio Cupai, Brazil); Eigenmann and Eigenmann, Proc. U.S. Nat. Mus., vol. 14, p. 71, 1891 (Amazon); Eigenmann and Bray, Ann. New York Acad. Sci., vol. 7, p. 624, 1894; Pellegrin, Mem. Soc. Zool. France vol. 16 p. 230, 1903 (Manaus); Regan, Ann. Mag. Nat. Hist. ser. 7, vol. 16, p. 440 1905 (Rio Cupai; Rio Negro; Teffé; Manaus.); Ihering, Revista Mus. Paulista, vol. 7, p. 336, 1907 (Amazonas; Rios Negro, Madeira, Xingu); Eigenmann, Repts. Princeton Univ. Exped. Patagonia, 1896–1899, vol. 3 Zool. pt. 4, p. 479, 1910 (Amazon and tributaries); Haseman Ann. Carnegie Mus., vol. 7, nos. 3, 4, p. 372, 1911 (Manaus, Santarem); Hegener, Blät. Aquar. Terr. vol. 47, no. 11, p. 241, 1937.

In addition to the references cited here Meinken *in* Holly, Meinken and Rachow (Die Aquarienfische in Wort und Bild, Liefurung, 75–76, pp. 769–773 1943) give numerous references for *Symphysodon*.

Specimens examined: USNM 179828, a single specimen, 76 mm. from tip of snout to midbase of caudal fin rays, collected at Manaus, Brazil in the Amazon River.

Description: Counts are recorded in tables 1 and 2 for this species. Although no significant differences in number of fin rays was found between *S. discus* and the other species, *S. discus* definitely has a fewer number of vertical scale rows from rear of head to caudal base, 44 instead of 50 to 61. The scales on the head above the eye reach to the edge of the bony orbit dorsally but not on the fleshy rim; the patch of free scales behind posterior edge of eye are lacking; scales on dorsal part of head do not reach quite to a line between the pairs of supraorbital pores; posterior pre-opercular row of scales reaches a little above the dorsal end of preopercular groove.

Symphysodon aequifasciata aequifasciata, photographed by Hilmar Hansen.

Color pattern: Background coloration of body composed of alternating horizontal light reddish-brown and bluish streaks, numbering about 15 to 18; these streaks beginning behind oper-culum and on forehead at midanterodorsal line, continue a some-what wavy course posteriorly, thence disappearing at base of median fins; the usual 9 vertical bars are present, three of which are dark blue, the others scarcely distinct; the first is a broad one through the eye to isthmus, next three very light tan, the fifth is a broad dark blue one, attaining its greatest intensity on lower midside of body but not reaching to base of anal fin; the next three are very light tan; the last is a broad bar across base of caudal fin sharply contrasting with general background coloration as do numbers one and five; the usual dark band on bases of dorsal and anal fins indistinct; distal parts of median fins light blue with scattered light blue spots; pectoral fin light blue; oblique light streaks on cheek, and two or three vertical ones on opercle; outer pelvic ray blue; other rays yellowish.

Symphysodon aequifasciata axelrodi photographed by Miloslav Kocar.

Remarks: Steindachner (Sitz Akad. Wiss. Wien vol. 71, p. 46–47, 1875) had two species of *Symphyosodon* because he mentions that in small specimens the vertical scale rows were 46 to 48, whereas in large specimens the scales numbered 52 to 56. This is exactly what I have found for *S. discus* and *S. aequifasciata* Pellegrin, the latter having the greater number of scales.

All of the species and subspecies, including the two new subspecies, are distinguished and diagnosed in the accompanying key.

SYMPHYSODON AEQUIFASCIATA AEQUIFASCIATA PELLEGRIN

Symphysodon discus aequifasciatus Pellegrin Mem. Soc. Zool. France, vol. 16, p. 230, 1903 (type locality, Lago Teffé and Santarem, Brazil).
Symphysodon discus Steindachner (in part) (Sitz. Akad. Wiss. Wien, vol. 71, p. 46–47, 1875 (Lago Teffé); Eigenmann, Repts. Princeton Univ. Exped. Patogonia 1896–1899, vol. 3, Zool. pt. 4, p. 479, 1910 (Santarem; Teffé); Ribeiro, Fauna Brasiliense, Arch. Mus. Nac. Rio de Janeiro, vol. 17, p. 69, fig., 1915 (Amazon and tributaries); Fowler, Mus. Hist. Nat. Javier Prado, Univ. Nac. Mayor San Marcos, Lima, p. 252, fig. 87, 1945 (Peruvian Amazon); Innes, Exotic Aquarium Fishes, color plate, p. 439, 1950 (Amazon); Axelrod and Schultz, Handbook of Tropical Aquarium Fishes, p. 655, color plate, 1955 (Amazon).

Specimens examined: USNM 179611, 104 specimens, 69 to 148 mm. collected in Lago Teffé, Brazil, by Harald Schultz.

Description: Certain counts and measurements are recorded in tables. Scales on head above the eye reach to bony edge of orbit but not on fleshy margin of eye; a patch of two or three isolated scales behind eye dorsally; posterior preopercular row of scales reaches above dorsal end of preopercular groove and is almost continuous with the patch of isolated scales.

Color pattern: Background coloration dark brownish green with nine dark brown vertical bars all of about the same intensity except last is darkest; these dark bars have the same positions as the homologous dark bars in the other species of *Symphysodon*. Basal three-fourths of dorsal and anal fins blackish, distally these fins are light olive green with scattered light spots basally; caudal fins translucent with scattered light spots; horizontal blackish streaks on head, dorsally on body and on dorsal fin, mostly absent on midsides, but distinct ventrally on anal fin. Alternating light blue and dark oblique streaks on cheek; three vertical, dark, bluish streaks on opercular; iris reddish-brown, pelvic dark green, outer ray blue, and tips of pelvic rays dark brown; pectoral fin translucent, its base dark green.

SYMPHYSODON AEQUIFASCIATA HARALDI,
new species

Symphysodon discus tarzoo Lyons, Tropicals Magazine, Holiday issue 1960, vol. 4, no. 3, pp. 6–10, 4 figs., Nov. 28, 1959 (Amazon in vicinity of Leticia (nomen nudum).)
Symphysodon discus, Meinken in Holly, Meinken and Rachow, Dis Aquarienfische in Wort and Bild, Lieferung 75–76; pp. 769–773; 41, 6, photographs, color drawing, 1943 (Biology of discus); Fowler, Mus. Hist. Nat. Univ. Nac. Mayor San Marcos, Lima p. 253, fig. 87, 1945 (Peruvian Amazon).

When an unknown or new aquarium fish is introduced to aquarium hobbyists and a name is printed such as the one Mr. Earl Lyons introduced for the blue discus, confusion and disagreement among those interested in scientific zoological nomenclature is likely to occur unless the rules of zoological nomenclature are followed. I have shown Dr. Curt Sabrosky, the article by Mr. Lyons and he agrees that the name *tarzoo* does not have nomenclatorial standing because the following two rules were not fulfilled as defined by the International Rules of Zoological Nomenclature and adopted at the 1927 Budapest Congress.

(1) After January 1, 1931, the specific name must have been published with a statement in which the author attempted to indicate differentiating characters or with a summary of characters which distinguish the species from other species, (2) the publication of a figure of the species with a scientific name does not meet these requirements.

Therefore, I must conclude that Mr. Lyons' article does not establish any scientific name.

To avoid confusion in the future in our Zoological Nomenclature it seems wise to describe as a new subspecies the blue discus according to the Rules of Zoological Nomenclature.

Holotype: USNM 179829, a specimen 117 mm. in standard length, collected at Benjamin Constant, Brazil, in the Amazon, by H. R. Axelrod and Harald Schultz.

Symphysodon aequifasciata haraldi in a color photograph of one of the actual fishes studied by Dr. Leonard Schultz in his determination of the species and subspecies of the genus *Symphysodon*. This photograph was taken by Dr. Herbert R. Axelrod from a fish he collected at Benjamin Constant, Brazil.

Description: Certain counts and measurements are recorded in tables 1 and 2. Scales on head above the eye reach to pores above eye but not quite to edge of bony orbit; a patch of two or three isolated scales behind eye dorsally; posterior preopercular row of scales reaches above dorsal end of preopercular groove and almost continuous with patch of scales; scales on dorsal part of head do not reach to the supraorbital pores.

Color Pattern: Background coloration of body brownish anteriorly, darker brown posteriorly; head purplish; head and body crossed with nine dark blue vertical bars, first and last darkest, first bar through eye across cheek to isthmus; second

S. aequifasciata axelrodi, the brown discus. Arend van den Nieuwenhuizen

Table 1. Counts recorded for the species and subspecies of *Symphysodon*.

NUMBER OF FIN RAYS

Species and subspecies	Dorsal									Anal										Pectoral					
	VIII	IX	X	29	30	31	32	33	34	VII	VIII	IX	26	27	28	29	30	31	32	ii	7	8	9	iii	iv
discus	—	1	—	—	—	1	—	—	—	1	—	—	—	—	—	1	—	—	—	2	2	—	—	—	2
aequifasciata aequifasciata	1	19	3	1	3	7	7	4	1	—	20	2	—	2	1	1	10	5	3	19	—	12	7	10	9
haraldi	—	1	—	—	—	1	—	—	—	—	1	—	—	—	—	1	—	—	—	2	—	2	—	—	2
axelrodi	1	20	7	—	6	14	7	7	—	2	21	5	2	1	7	3	9	4	2	29	—	20	9	15	14

NUMBER OF PORES IN LATERAL LINE

Species and subspecies	Anterior lateral line						Caudal lateral line					Total pores								
	18	19	20	21	22	23	10	11	12	13	14	28	29	30	31	32	33	34	35	36
discus	—	1	—	—	—	—	—	—	1	—	—	—	—	—	1	—	—	—	—	—
aequifasciata aequifasciata	1	4	4	8	4	2	1	4	7	9	2	—	—	1	3	6	4	4	4	1
haraldi	—	—	1	—	—	—	—	—	—	1	—	—	—	—	—	—	1	—	—	—
axelrodi	2	5	8	5	7	2	4	8	9	8	—	1	3	3	10	7	4	1	—	—

Table 2.   Counts recorded for the species and subspecies of *Symphysodon*.

Species and subspecies	Number of vertical scale rows from upper edge of opercular opening in a straight line to base of caudal fin.																		NUMBER OF VERTEBRAE										
																			Abdominal			Caudal				Total			
	44	45	46	47	48	49	50	51	52	53	54	55	56	57	58	59	60	61	12	13	14	17	18	19	20	30	31	32	33
discus																													
Steindachner 1	—	—	—	—	—	—	—	—	—	—	—	—	—	—	—	—	—	—	—	1	—	1	—	—	—	1	—	—	—
(1875)[1]	—	—	x	x	x	—	—	—	—	—	—	—	—	—	—	—	—	—	—	—	—	—	—	—	—	—	—	—	—
aequifasciata																													
aequifasciata	—	—	—	—	—	—	—	—	2	1	5	4	3	4	1	1	—	1	1	13	—	—	9	2	1	—	10	3	—
haraldi	—	—	—	—	—	—	—	—	—	1	—	—	—	—	—	—	—	—	—	1	—	—	1	—	—	—	1	—	—
axelrodi	—	—	—	—	—	—	2	2	4	2	4	4	2	1	2	—	—	—	1	14	2	1	15	1	—	1	14	2	—

Counts from literature

from spiny dorsal origin to upper edge of opercle; third across base of pectoral fin to base of pelvic fin; next four across body; next to last from rear edge of dorsal fin base across caudal pe-

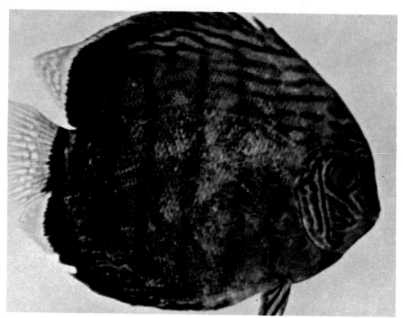

Symphysodon aequifasciata haraldi from Benjamin Constant, Brazil and photographed by Harald Schultz within eight hours of its capture. According to Dr. Axelrod, the scales were rubbed off the sides when the fish was carried to Schultz in a gasoline can that had only three inches of water for the seven inch high fish.

duncle to rear edge of base of anal fin; last dark bar almost black across base of caudal fin rays; basal three-fourths of dorsal and anal fins dark blackish-purple that blends in with the background coloration of body; distal areas of soft dorsal and anal fins light yellowish with scattered light spots mostly basally; caudal fin translucent also with scattered light spots basally; pelvic fin dark brown, outer ray blue, distally the tips of rays are pinkish; pectoral fin purple, its base brown; horizontal wavy blue streaks irregularly interrupted, cover the entire body, except breast and behind head, and distal parts of median fins; forehead with four or five blue horizontal streaks, two oblique blue streaks below eye and two vertical blue bars on operculum.

Dr. Eduard Schmidt photo of *Symphysodon aequifasciata aequifasciata*.

In alcohol the purple bars preserve as dark brown and the blue streaks almost completely disappear.

Remarks: This new subspecies was named *haraldi* in honor of Mr. Harald Schultz, Sao Paulo, Brazil, who has collected numerous new and rare South American fishes.

SYMPHYSODON AEQUIFASCIATA AXELRODI,
new species

Holotype: USNM 179831, a specimen 105 mm. in standard length collected at Belem, Brazil, Amazon River by Herbert Axelrod.

Paratypes: USNM 179609, Rio Urubu, nine specimens, 105 to 122 mm. in standard length, collected by Herbert R. Axelrod and Harald Schultz.

USNM 179610, Rio Urubu, 48 specimens, 75 to 139 mm. in standard length, collected by Herbert R. Axelrod and Harald Schultz.

Description: Certain counts and measurements are recorded in tables 1 and 2. Scales on head above the eye reach to edge of bony orbit but not to fleshy margin of eye; no isolated patch of scales behind eye; posterior preopercular row of scales does not reach to dorsal end of preopercular groove; scales on dorsal part of head do not reach to the supraorbital pores.

Color Pattern: Background coloration light yellowish-brown to dark brown, overlaid with nine vertical bars, the first through eye is dark purplish-brown to blackish and the last through base of

caudal fin rays blackish, these two (first and last) notably darker than the other seven, all of which are light purplish to purplish-brown; the second at origin of spiny dorsal fin ends at upper edge of opercular opening; third passes through base of pectoral fin thence ending at base of pelvic fin; the next four across body; the next to last vertical bar occurs on caudal peduncle and extends from rear edge of base of dorsal fin to that of the anal fin. Soft dorsal fin and soft anal fin basally with a broad dark purplish band that is continuous with the dark crossbar at base of caudal peduncle and contrasts notably with the light brown background color of body; soft dorsal and anal fins distally light olive, with scattered lighter spots mostly basally; pelvic fin reddish brown with distal tips of rays yellow or orange; anal spines blue, mem-

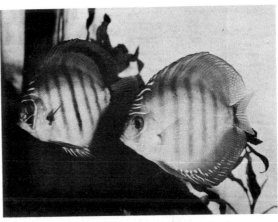

The discus in the Mueller-Schmida photo appear to be young *axelrodi*; photographer G. J. M. Timmerman identifies those opposite as *S. aequifasciata haraldi.*

branes brownish; pectoral fin light blue to light purplish; bases of pectoral rays purple; operculum dark purple; iris red; forehead with about four horizontal light blue streaks; anal fin with blue streaks basally.

In alcohol the vertical purple bars preserve as dark bars against a lighter brownish background.

Named in honor of Herbert R. Axelrod who collected most of the specimens used in this study. This new subspecies is diagnosed in the accompanying key.

Brown discus and eggs.

Brown discus, *Symphysodon aequifasciata axelrodi* are characterized by their uniform body color, the relatively even vertical stripes and the lack of blue horizontal streaks on their bodies when compared to the other species and subspecies.

DISCUSFISH ARE SPAWNED

(From *Tropical Fish Hobbyist*, February, 1957)

In 1933 aquarists saw the first living specimens of the fabled Pompadour Fish, *Symphysodon discus*. Up until that time its magnificent beauty was only a fable because Dr. Heckel, when he first described the fish and gave it its name in 1840 (Ann. Wien. Mus. Naturges., 2:333, pl. 30, figs. 21 and 22), emphasized with illustrations that this was a magnificent spectacle of nature.

Once it had reached the aquarium market, a mad scramble for the first specimens occurred and their price jumped from a mere $50.00 each to upwards of $650.00 per pair! Since that importation, over 67,000 specimens of all sizes and ages have been imported from the Rio Negro system in South America and everyone who bought a pair hoped against hope that they might be fortunate enough to propagate the species and win fame and fortune in a highly competitive field.

The first successful spawning of this highly prized species was accomplished by Mr. W. T. Dodd in 1949. He had wonderful success with a single pair, raising as many as 200 fry per biweekly spawning, but his pair died and he was unable to repeat his success with other fish.

During the next seven years others have successfully bred the discusfish only to have the parents eat the eggs. When the parents were removed immediately after spawning, great difficulty was experienced in raising the young. To this date very few breeders have been able to raise fry without the aid of the parents . . . and now we know why!

As the fry grow out of their yolk-absorbing stage three days after the four day hatching period, they were observed to actually pick microscopic infusorians off the slimy covering of their parents' bodies. They utilized this food source for a few days and gradually grew to the point where they could eat newly-hatched brine shrimp and small cyclops.

BREEDING THE BROWN DISCUS (SYMPHYSODON AEQUIFASCIATA AXELRODI)

BY GUENTHER KELLER

A city child, spending a vacation in the country, is charmed at his first view of a sow suckling her lively little piglets. Something similar is felt by the novice aquarist when first he gets acquainted with how discus fish care for their offspring, and the way discus babies are fed by their parents does not differ too much from that of the pink little pigs.

When the conversation turns to breeding discus, reference is generally made to the brown discus, *Symphysodon aequifasciata axelrodi*. The green discus (*Symphysodon aequifasciata aequifasciata*), and the blue discus (*Symphysodon aequifasciata haraldi*) are really a little bit more colorful, but they also are rarer and costlier.*

If it loses out in a comparison of its colors with those of its prettier relatives, the brown discus can still represent a feast for the eyes when kept and illuminated in the correct manner. The red fins and blue stripes should receive top lighting to do them justice. But since generally we purchase home-bred or imported young fish, we generally have to be patient for about a year before the fish show their true worth.

A Fish Which Poses Great Demands

We have to keep the discus in surroundings that are as true to nature as possible. Despite the fact that this is no new discovery at all, most discus still end up in community tanks. And to get them to spawn there is pure coincidence indeed. If we want to breed them systematically, we have to buy a minimum of five young fish from among which we can then choose the "correct" pair later on. The fish should be kept by themselves in a larger tank (from 50 gallons up). This isolation in a large tank is the best way we have of protecting them against fish diseases.

*There are two species of discus: *Symphysodon aequifasciata* and *Symphysodon discus*, the true discus. The sub-species *Symphysodon aequifasciata axelrodi* is the one most often found in fanciers' tanks.

This is the famous breeding pair of *Symphysodon aequifasciata aequifasciata* which Dr. Eduard Schmidt-Focke received from Kyle Swegles when he visited Chicago. The dark fish on the left is the female (see her photograph with fry on pages 68 and 69). The male on the right is also illustrated on page 45 and 77. Photo by Dr. Eduard Schmidt-Focke.

It is unimportant for rearing the fish whether we set up the tank as a "sanitary" one (without bottom covering) or as an "ornamental" one. One thing we have to pay attention to is that the breeding tank should be kept as clean as possible, and I personally consider the clean-bottomed tank unavoidable for successful breeding. Confusing discussions about the correct water have been, and still are, going on. For a long time the specialists contended that keeping the fish successfully could only be done in soft water. It has been demonstrated, however, that keeping, and even breeding, is not impossible in medium-hard to pronouncedly-hard water (20 DH and more).

It has to be admitted, though, that things work out much better in soft to medium-hard water. It is difficult to establish an upper limit, since this is influenced by many factors. In practice it should be placed around 8 to 10° DH. Water that is still softer is doubtlessly more favorable, though. On the one hand this corresponds to the fishes' natural habitat, on the other hand soft

This is an almost mature offspring from the pair shown spawning on page 65. The fish were bred by Dr. Eduard Schmidt-Focke, who gave them to Dr. Rolf Geisler, where they were photographed by Wolfgang Bechtle.

water is easier to change around towards the qualities of natural water by filtering it through peat moss. Peat moss undoubtedly holds the first place as a filtering medium. Experiments at keeping discus in tanks in which the water was filtered through gravel, coal or ozone have always demonstrated that the fish felt best and showed their prettiest colors in peat-filtered water. Dr. R. Geisler, the internationally famous water chemist, has proved the favorable effect of peat in numerous experiments. By the way: be careful really to use acid, white peat. Test a sample of the peat, aerating it before measuring. Acid peat will still deliver a pH value of 4 or less in such cases.

The size of the peat filter depends on the quality of the peat, the quantity of water, and the hardness factors of same. Make your own experiments. My own experience shows that discus will withstand very acid surroundings; pH values of 4.2 to 4.5 were taken in stride without any objection. A pH value of 5.5 to 6.5 is still absolutely satisfactory.

I have observed that the young specimens not only possess the largest appetites, but also are not as choosy as full-grown fish. Once they have got used to a kind of food, they will keep eating it up to advanced ages. Older fish, to the contrary, may pose difficulties, therefore we should put feeding on a wide basis from the beginning, making the diet as varied as possible.

Sound young discus will eat all kinds of mosquito larvae, tubifex, white worms, *Daphnia*, fruit fly larvae, small crustaceans, beef heart, spleen, and will not even shun the different dried foods. To all this I still add a food with an agar-agar base which will be described further on.

In my opinion it is important to feed as varied a diet as possible, not only in order to offer the fishes nutritious meals, but especially to break them of the habit of one kind of food only, which may be exactly one of those that are costly or hard to get in quantities. Even if you have discovered a *Daphnia* pond of large yield or a hole chockful of mosquito larvae, intersperse the feedings with different foods, so that the fish will not balk later on when no more *Daphnia* or mosquito larvae are available. I have also registered great success with freeze-dried foods. If you are conscientious to keep and feed your fish efficiently, you will be astonished at their quick growth and liveliness.

Things are not Always Peaceful

Bickering will appear among the young discus fishes. Could it be the establishing of a "pecking" order? It can hardly be fights for a "range" for discus do not defend firm home sites—they generally roam in swarms through the tank. The provocations start mainly at feeding time—the highest-ranking defending the lump of tubifex against all comers. One thing, though, has become clear: This warlike behavior should not be taken in consideration when sexing the fish. In previous publications the opinion was defended that the aggressor who carries out the buttings, is of the male sex, and the fish which gives way, while its body takes on a stripe design meanwhile, is a female. This is by no means the case; for if we take out the "highest-ranking" fish, the behavior of the other specimens towards one another changes. In most cases the "highest-ranking" discus is a male, but I have seen exceptions. Besides the genital papilla there is no sure sign that will permit differentiating the sexes. One thing I was able to observe is that in mated pairs the males were slightly larger than the females, but with single specimens, or when we are facing a school, this uncertain feature will of course not be sufficient to ascertain the sex by the simple expedient of size.

Nuptial Preparations

We always have to wait until a pair have found each other. They will let *you* know that a blessed event is in store. We have to watch the fishes closely, though: buttings become scarcer and the area of the head as well as of the tail fin takes on a somewhat blackish hue. When the fish pass each other they bow their heads while opening and closing the tail fins. Soon after this, "shaking" starts, and the pair begins looking for a spawning site. We should help them in this and offer them an adequate spawning substratum. Discus are quite inventive when it is the question of a breeding place—they spawn on broad-leaved plastic or real plants, rocks, thermostats, slate, heaters, glass panes—but so far the best results have always been obtained with an inverted red clay flower pot. On this the fish find a centrally located and comfortable spawning site which they accept thankfully. My own best successes were obtained with a funnel-shaped vase of baked clay which was a little smaller in diameter. The slanted conical sides and the lower rim proved to be especially practical: wriggling

haraldi discus, with eggs deposited on a flower pot.

Dr. Eduard Schmidt photo.

alevins which fall down are always able to catch themselves on the inclined surface, or at least on the rim, where the parents immediately find them again.

But first the selected spot is cleaned by the pair in a cooperation, in the well-known cichlid manner.

After two or three days we will be able to watch the spawning in the evening hours.†

---

†But before things are ready there are still some critical stages to overcome. If the fish are supposed to care for their young and to watch their eggs, it is advisable to remove all other fishes. Once Discus have gotten used to certain surroundings, they are apt to react very disturbedly if they are moved to another tank for breeding. If the nursery tanks have been set up for breeding conditions, though (without covering on the bottom, and stocked with flower pots), and the fish find the same potentialities in them, then the spawning activities may continue without interruption. With changed conditions, however, pauses have been observed of up to six weeks.

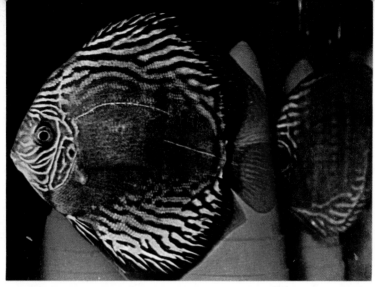

haraldi discus among flower pots, guarding and fanning their eggs. Dr. Eduard Schmidt photo.

Generally the fish spell each other at the pot. First the female releases her eggs, then the male fertilizes them. If the pair is well mated, sometimes both partners slide up the pot wall simultaneously and carry out the act of spawning together. Good layings contain about 200 eggs, but only in very rare cases do all of them hatch: 175 reared fry from one brood was the record, as far as I know. I myself succeeded in getting 157 fish. But from these I had to exclude a few "belly-sliders."

The Overworked Discus Parents

If the parents watch their spawn, and fan it steadily with well-oxygenated water by means of their pectorals, at a water temperature of 86°F we can count upon the fry hatching within 60 hours. The eggs do not seem sensitive to light. In my tank they are immediately below the fluorescent light fixture, with floating plants as their only protection. Furthermore full lighting does not seem to bother the parents while spawning, which nearly always takes place during the evening hours.

When the egg shells burst, the fry are generally sucked free by the parents, who carry them to another spot. There they are hung up by a mucous thread provided by a gland in the head. Normally the parents also fan the fry, and each baby fish that falls down is immediately caught with their mouths and spit back to its rightful place. Especially during this stage it becomes most important to keep the tank irreproachably clean. In a tank where there is a covering layer of sand or gravel on the bottom, and "mulm" to boot, it turns out impossible for the parents to detect baby fishes that slide off, and we are bound to lose a great part of the offspring. At this moment the water, too, should be crystal clear, with nearly all bacteria eliminated through filtering through peat moss. There is no objection to turning off the light during nighttime.

I have observed that the young move very little in darkness, and therefore there is little danger of their falling off at this time.

During this period the parents which are caring for their young eat very little and show a reluctance to leave their brood alone. It is advisable to feed them freeze-dried brine shrimp or tubifex during this time. If the food moves in the open water, the parents easily become irritated, and mistake *Daphnia* or mosquito larvae for their own young. I have often seen how they were continually spitting the food animals into the middle of their brood.

"Daddy" Suckles Too

After another 60 hours the fry are already free-swimming, and the last, decisive stage of rearing them starts. The first fugitives are again and again caught by the parent fish and spit back in place. But soon the poor parents will find that they are unable to cope with all these delinquent young. Little by little the whole brood appears on the bodies of their parents and begin to graze off the skin secretion. It looks as if the grown-ups were suckling their babies. From now on father and mother lead their offspring alternately through the tank, watching out for straying offspring. Normally they gather the fry together in the evening, spitting them on the flower pot again, where they really stick during the first night. But I verified again and again that this never worked out too well, and that at least part of the brood persisted in adhering to the body of "daddy" or "mommy," respectively swimming away from the pot. After the aquarium lamp had been turned off, I saw many fry lost and floundering around in the tank, and the next day the total number was much smaller. For this reason I leave a weak light on, directed like a spot-light on the flower pot during the first night after free-swimming. Thus the parents are able to watch their brood, and conversely the babies

Danny DiCoco uses foster mothers, like this brown discus, *Symphysodon a. axelrodi*, since some parents are good breeders but bad baby feeders. Photo by Dr. Herbert R. Axelrod.

can find their way back to their parents. This method has shown good results and has diminished the losses.

It is always an imposing sight to watch a pair of discus sailing majestically through a tank, surrounded by a flock of young which dance around them like a swarm of gnats. On the sixth day after the fry are swimming free I start to feed freshly-hatched brine shrimp. Despite the fact that the baby fish could eat them sooner, it would not be useful to give them this diet earlier, for they eat only what comes in front of their mouths. The link to the skin secretion, and therewith to the parents, is still so strong that at this stage they do not prey on food. They free themselves from the parents only after a week, and it is only then that additional food becomes really important. After an initial diet of *Artemia*, I change over to microworms, cyclops, chopped tubifex, and larger foods. As a rule I leave the brood with their parents for four weeks. Those young which I tried separating earlier from the parents turned out considerably less well-developed. The influence of the skin secretion upon growth is so evident that we should necessarily permit the small ones this source of strength as long as possible.

As soon as they have become independent, the water values may be changed without danger.

S. aequifasciata axelrodi, the brown discus. Photo by Helmut Pinter.

S. aequifasciata haraldi opposite.

The Best-hated Parasite

But it is not always that breeding discus takes its course as normally as described above. Difficulties often start with the rearing of the fish. Numerous discus fanciers have observed that their fish suddenly started eating very little, turned to not ingesting anything at all, and died slowly. And generally they saw mucous-intermixed and light-colored excrement. Now and then a mouthful of food was still taken, but then the fish were beyond saving. Lately scientists, especially Dr. Schubert of the Zoological Institute of Hohenheim, Germany, have tracked the cause of the disease; in most cases a flagellate, *Octomitus*, is to blame. Discus fish seem to be especially prone to such parasite attacks. Under inexpert treatment the parasite is apt to multiply very quickly. It attacks mainly the inner organs, especially the intestinal tract. The consequence: severe digestive disturbances, generally ending fatally. What can be done to fight this? My own practice leads me to give the following advice:

1. Always keep your discus to themselves in order to save them from the constant source of infection represented by other fish species.
2. Change part of your water frequently.
3. Keep the bottom of the tank as clean as possible. *Octomitus* is an excrement dweller and able to survive there for rather long periods. Constant re-infection prevents the fish from getting well.

The only hope for an effective cure is to administer adequate medication with the food. But the correct remedy has not been discovered, and infected fish often stop eating.

I can suggest a method which may possibly succeed in reaching the parasites through feeding. I have for some time now been using a home-made food based on agar-agar for the rearing of baby discus.

It consists of calf liver, spleen, fresh-water crustaceans, deep-frozen mosquito larvae, several commercial dried foods, and additions of vitamins. All this is beaten to a pulp and blended with agar-agar. Young discus relish this jelly, and the mix apparently causes them to grow much quicker than if raised only on tubifex and *Daphnia*. Agar-agar as food substratum is slated to become the carrier for antibiotics§ and other medicines.

When Parents Eat Their Offspring

Most mishaps encountered in breeding discus fish take place during the act of spawning. Often one or both of the parents eat the eggs while they are being laid or immediately thereafter. As far as I know, this is something that cannot be remedied. Generally, though, this egg cannibalism stops after a couple of spawnings, but often the fish continue as notorious egg robbers for ever. I once had to watch a male in my tank eating 43 successive egg releases, despite the fact that in each case I gave him a different set-up. This fish was useless for breeding. The female, however, raised many further broods with another mate. In such cases the first premise is to show patience and—whenever possible—to mate the right couples. Often this is not easy, but I have one pair that has now been spawning for eleven months, and raising each brood—with one unimportant exception.

Some fanciers complain that they eventually have parent fish which do not secrete any food substance from the skin. No breeding attempt of mine has ever failed due to this problem. The fry have always found food on their parents, even when the gray film was hardly noticeable on them. On the other hand there are also cases in which the skin secretion is produced in huge amounts.

Several broods were also reared by only one fish, the male, which claimed the sole right of representation. And in every one of these cases the father was perfectly able to feed his young, despite the fact that there were over a hundred of them.

In spite of all these findings, one will hardly ever be able to develop the art of breeding discus fish into a routine, for this fish is not yet sufficiently adapted to the conditions of our tanks. But if we pay a little attention to its vital needs, the discus will grant us a lot of joy . . . and profit!

§Antibiotics are germ preventing or germ killing substances—excellent remedies against infectious diseases. The best known antibiotics are: Penicillin, Streptomycin, Aureomycin, Chloromycetin, and Tetracycline.

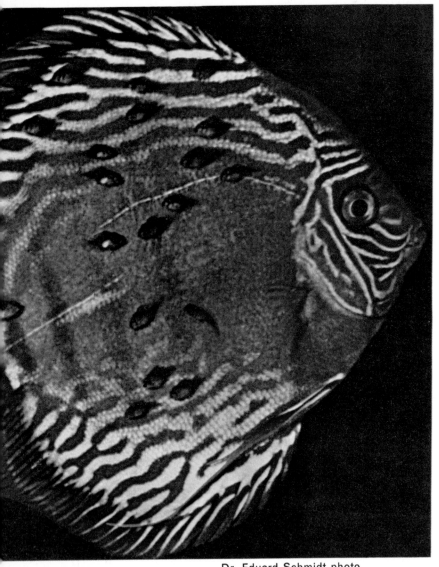

Dr. Eduard Schmidt photo.

S. aequifasciata haraldi fry subsist upon parental exudations.

Both parents tend the eggs, guarding and fanning them, and removing any attacked by fungus. Dr. Eduard Schmidt photo.

While tending newly-hatched fry (on leaf below), discus parents are ever alert and no visitors are welcomed. Gerhard Budich photo.

During the period in which fry subsist upon parental exudations, they usually pass en masse from one parent to the other. Gerhard Budich photo.

Whether the skin secretions or tiny organisms populating the slime serve principally as food for fry is not certain. Dr. Eduard Schmidt photo.

The female *Symphysodon aequifasciata aequifasciata* with her parasitic fry. This is the same fish shown on the facing page and is the darker fish to the left in the photograph on page 52. Photo by Dr. Eduard Schmidt-Focke.

Though discus fry subsist upon parental secretions for only a week or a few days longer, growth is rapid, as shown in the photos by Gerhard Budich here and on page 74.

Hilmar Hansen photographed the brown discus, *Symphysodon aequi-fasciata axelrodi* at the beautiful aquarium in Berlin under the direction of the world famous Director Werner Schroeder. On the top of the facing page we see another brown discus, *S.a. axelrodi*, whose stripes were not evident at the time of the photo. A few minutes later, after being frightened by the strobe light, the stripes appeared and the dorsal fin collapsed. On the bottom of the facing page is a true discus, *Symphysodon discus*, clearly showing the three vertical stripes which differentiate it from the sub-species of *Symphysodon aequifasciata*. Harald Schultz' photo also shows the horizontal streaking on *S. discus*, which covers most of its body, making it the most beautiful discus to say nothing of its cost.

The fry opposite are large enough to snap up small aquatic animals that approach too near; soon they will begin darting after such prey, and before long will become independent of parents for food and protection. There are always some individuals who never get the word, and obviously some of the fry above have missed the signal to change feeding stations. Gerhard Budich photos.

This photograph of *Symphysodon aequifasciata aequifasciata* shows a wild fish from the western-most range of the genus *Symphysodon*. The red spots on the lower sides of the fish, also found on angelfish, *Pterophyllum,* and *Cichlasoma severum* occur only on fishes found far up the Amazon River system at least 2,000 miles or more from the Atlantic Ocean. Photo by Hilmar Hansen, Berlin Aquirium.

IMPORTED DISEASES

BY DR. GOTTFRIED SCHUBERT
Photos by the author
(From *Tropical Fish Hobbyist*, November, 1969)

Fish are not free of parasites just because they were swimming in their native habitat a short time ago. Fish bred in Hong Kong or Singapore (they are sold as "imports," too) may have diseases not found in the USA.

Symphysodon aequifasciata aequifasciata in spawning dress. This is the same male shown in the photograph on page 45. Photo by Dr. Eduard Schmidt-Focke.

A short while ago *Pterophyllum scalare* brought an unwelcome guest with it, a hair-worm, *Capillaria pterophylli*. This parasite lives in the midgut of the angelfish. The females reach a length of about 2 cm but are only 0.07 mm in diameter. Males are much smaller. If you have good eyes you may sometimes see such a worm hanging like a fine thread out of the anus of the fish. The females lay eggs which, together with the feces, sink to the bottom and are eaten by other fish, which in turn will harbor these worms. Those who own a microscope will easily detect the eggs in fresh

A back view of the inch-long discus feeding from and deriving protection from their father. As the discus fry get bigger and bigger they eat less from their parents than from newly hatched brine shrimp or freeze-dried shrimp offered by the breeder . . .

. . . A front view showing the inch-long fry grazing off the front end of the father. As the slime diminishes, it seems to diminish from the tail to the head as the school congregates towards the head of the fish when feeding.

Symphysodon discus

This young adult is about four inches in diameter and has a considerable amount of growing ahead. Dr. Herbert R. Axelrod photo.

S. aequifasciata axelrodi photographed by Hilmar Hansen, Berlin Aquarium.

Dr. Herbert R. Axelrod photo of the discus named honoring him.

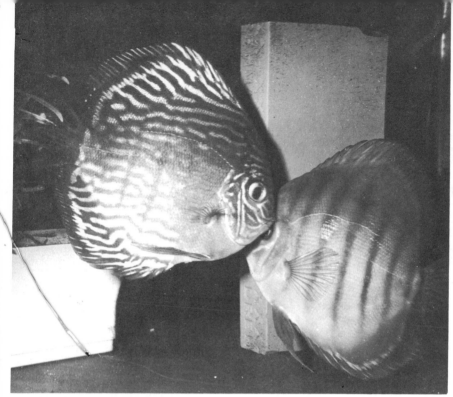

Dr. Axelrod's photographs show the DiCoco spawning of a hybrid *Symphysodon aequifasciata haraldi* X *Symphysodon discus* with a brown discus, *Symphysodon a. axelrodi* . . .

feces. They have a very peculiar shape and it is nearly impossible to mistake them for something else.

Today a high percentage of all angelfish in our tanks are infected with hair-worms. But other fish may get these worms, too. Especially endangered are, of course, all fishes which take their food from the bottom, as such fishes easily swallow worm eggs. Therefore the different species of *Corydoras* are frequently found infected. Fishes that live in the middle zone of our tanks, like tetras, rarely show *Capillaria* infection. Those snatching their prey from the surface of the water are never infected.

A few hair-worms in a fish usually don't matter much, but if there are thousands of them they may kill their host. This occurs rarely, so *Capillaria* is mostly unknown to hobbyists. But we ought to watch the future, because the different species of the genus *Symphysodon* (discus) seem to be very sensitive to hair-

. . . Once the pair laid their eggs, they all fungused. As far as is known, no one has successfully crossed two hybrids together, though crossing the sub-species or species from their native habitat presents no problem.

worms. *Symphysodon* kept in the same tank with angelfish are nearly always infected. In freshly imported *Symphysodon* I have never found *Capillaria*. *Symphysodon* reacts strongly to hair-worm infections, even if there are but a few worms. Another disease found in a high percentage of all *Symphysodon* turns worse by a simultaneous worm infection. A small flagellate with the Latin name *Spironucleus* is present in all *Symphysodon* living in their natural habitat. Usually this parasite occurs in small numbers only and does little harm. But under the less than optimal conditions of captivity the flagellates multiply enormously, and soon there are millions and millions of them. They primarily live in the gut but may spread to other organs. This wandering is advantageous to *Capillaria*. The worms are inclined to puncture the intestinal wall and thus open pathways for *Spironucleus*. An infection of the kidney by *Spironucleus* means death to *Symphysodon*.

The so-called "red discus," *Symphysodon aequifasciata aequifasciata,* with red spots which indicates it comes from near Peru or Colombia. Under Gro-lux light, this fish appears almost solid red. Photo by Gerhard Marcuse.

Certain parasites are harmless in our tanks. If I dissect a *Symphysodon* I can tell whether the fish was bred in captivity or caught in its native river. All wild *Symphysodon* have larvae of flukes in their organs, but these parasites cannot infect our tanks. The fish is but an intermediate host for the fluke. The adult parasite lives in a fish-eating animal (bird, crocodile, bigger fish). In tanks there is no chance for the fluke to find its final host and become an adult animal.

How could we prevent importing diseases together with our fish? I see two ways: we can appeal to the dealers. They usually don't import single fish but quite a number of a given species at any one time. It seems possible to dissect and check, let us say, one

Symphysodon aequifasciata aequifasciata, the green discus, photographed by Harald Schultz shortly after it was taken from Lake Tefé.

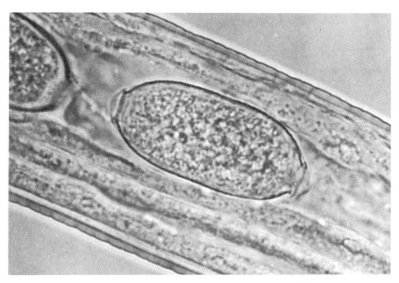

Eggs of the hair-worm, *Capillaria pterophylli*.

Dr. Gottfried Schubert photographs.

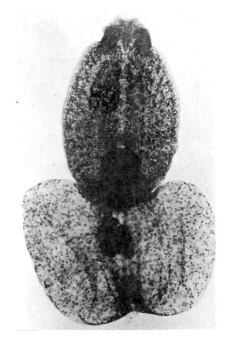

Larva of fluke found in many
imported discus.

out of a hundred. If it proves necessary the fish must be treated or even destroyed. But since this involves loss of money, I am not very hopeful about it. The other possibility seems more favorable. The breeders among us could take care of it. In many instances it is possible to breed healthy offspring from diseased parents. A little knowledge of the diseases the fish suffer from is necessary to achieve this. Since many hobbyists have turned into veritable chemists and engineers in order to have fine fish in their tanks, why shouldn't they become amateur veterinarians, too?

THE DELICATE DISCUS

BY DR. GOTTFRIED SCHUBERT

Breeders who are successful in propagating discus are considered by most hobbyists as master aquarists. What makes the king of freshwater aquarium fishes difficult to keep and breed is that the discus demands royal treatment. He prefers not to share his domain; he may perhaps be content in the company of dukes such as angelfishes, but even they are not wholly acceptable tankmates, and more active fishes are disconcerting as well as a dangerous source of contagion.

The king is particular about water conditions, and he prefers a varied diet. Soft, slightly acid water is to the royal taste. In the land of his origin, the water occupied by discus is sometimes below 1 DH, and that provided by the aquarist should be no harder than 5 DH. It is true that healthy discus show no indication of distress in water that is very hard indeed; they may even spawn in it, but embryonic fry will not develop to the point of emerging from the eggs.

It is also true that some discus keepers feed only tubifex worms through winter months without apparent detriment to the appetite or health of their discus. Even so, variation of diet is desirable since no single food can long supply the essential elements to keep the fishes in health.

The major difficulties facing the discus keeper are parasites and diseases. It is nearly impossible to acquire discus that are free from parasites. All of the imported ones that I have checked were

S. aequifasciata axelrodi from Rio Urubu, Brazil, Harald Schultz photo, and below a year-old brown discus photographed by Hilmar Hansen, Berlin Aquarium.

Axelrod found this discus, *Symphysodon aequifasciata aequifasciata,* in the Rio Purus; below the same fish as shown on page 85.

parasitically infested. In natural waters, discus seem not to be seriously harmed by these parasites, but their ravages and disease are often fatal to captive fishes. Fortunately tank-bred discus are free of many parasitic worms, the larval forms of which are nearly always found in wild discus. Other animals in natural habitat are hosts to these worms in certain stages of their development and any brought into the aquarium soon die out in the absence of these hosts.

A threat to captive discus is *Spironucleus* found in all discus, usually in the gut but sometimes also in other organs. Fish do not seem to suffer severely when infested by only a few thousands of these flagellates but their numbers can increase into the millions. In my opinion, formed through dissecting hundreds of discus, 90% of deaths among these fishes are caused by *Spironucleus*.

Dissection is not necessary to disclose serious infestation by this parasite. Milky-white feces is an indicator. If freshly dropped feces is picked up with a pipette, microscopic examination (magnification 300 times) will likely reveal the presence of these flagellates in huge numbers. So long as the parasites are restricted to the intestine, they are not usually dangerous, but the situation worsens when they invade other organs such as the gall bladder, liver, and kidneys.

How the parasites disperse to these organs is not known. Some scientists are of the opinion that they penetrate the walls of tissues while others think that travel is by way of the blood stream or through other organic passages. Parasites found in the kidneys are usually few in number but small crystals are formed in the tubules as a result and these blockages impair the function of the organs. The gills of fish can perform part of the necessary excretion, but in time the formation of crystals prevents this action of the gills and death soon follows.

At the Zoological Institute, Hohenheim University, a large number of discus were kept for study of this condition. I touched the water one day while feeding and discovered that the temperature had risen because of a thermostatic malfunction. Corrections were made and I thought no more about the occurrence until I killed a fish a few days later to show the flagellates to a colleague. There were none, nor were there any in two other fishes that were dissected, whereas all had previously been heavily infested.

Discusfishes darken as they reach advanced age and are sometimes nearly black at time of death. G. J. M. Timmerman photo.

We began experiments at the institute and a successful breeder conducted others to determine whether or not high water temperatures would eliminate the parasites without harming fishes. It was found that discus could endure 104° for only a few hours but tolerated 100° for several days and were comfortable at 95° temperature. The parasites could not survive longer than three days at 100°, and at the safer 95° temperature none persisted at the end of a week.

Infestations of Malawi cichlids at the Stuttgart Zoo led to other experiments since these fishes could not withstand such high temperatures, and we found that four milligrams (.24 grains) of metronidazol per gallon of water was an effective chemical control within a period of five to seven days.

In checking the feces for presence of this parasite, eggs of the hair-worm, *Capillaria pterophylli*, may be discovered. These worms

Young adult brown discus photographed in Czechoslovakia by Miloslav Kocar, and on facing page an attractive red discus photographed by Günter Keller.

These photographs were taken from the German aquarium magazine "Aquarienmagazin" and illustrate discus in various colors which depart from the norm. Dr. Axelrod rejects the deep red discus as a non-normal fish which is either a sport or has been dyed. Axelrod claims this fish doesn't exist in nature.

too are not dangerous in limited numbers but they anchor themselves to the intestinal wall and may thus cause wounds through which *Spironucleus* may easily pass to reach other organs. Discus are seldom host to the hair-worm but angelfish are usually infested. Housing angels and discus together is therefore poor policy as the danger to discus is compounded by double infestation. (Angels seem to be rather resistant to *Spironucleus*, but may be treated as discus for control.)

Hobbyists encounter problems, particularly with older discus, related to a disease of unknown source. It has been variously ascribed to tuberculosis, *Spironucleus*, *Ichthyosporidium*, and other organisms. Here it is known as puff disease, in America as hole-in-the-head disease, and is described as distinguised by the emergence of small, white worms (actually a discharge of pus). Only in early stages of the malady is treatment successful. Acriflavine is sometimes effective, but ecridine-lactate is far more reliable.

To treat, prepare a solution of 100 milligrams of ecridine-lactate in 100 milliliters (1 part in 1000) of boiling water. Cotton is dipped into the cooled solution and the yellow liquid is applied by gently touching the infected spots of the netted fish, being careful to keep the medication from reaching the gills. Normally the white puffs will clear within forty-eight hours and not reappear for a year or more.

HOLE-IN-THE-HEAD DISEASE

(From the T. F. H. book *Cichlids*)
BY ROBERT J. GOLDSTEIN, Ph.D.

An all too common affliction of discus fish is the so-called discus disease or *hole-in-the-head disease*. The cause of this disease remains unknown to this day. It has variously been reported as due to protozoa, fungi, worms, and bacteria. I have examined a number of such diseased fishes, and have come up with some observations, but no firm conclusions. First, I have never found *Ichthyophonus* or known pathogenic bacteria in the carcasses. There are no worms. What looks like a worm is actually pus forming a string and flowing in the current around the fish's head. I have found what appears to be some kind of fungus in the livers of some of the fish, but it is unclear how this could possible be related to the disease of the head, and I tend to consider it unrelated to discus disease, unless it is a predisposing factor (perhaps weakening them to invasion by something else). The holes in the head follow the general course of the frontal lateral line system, and may indeed be the result of infection of the nervous system. If this is the case, then the cause should be either bacterial or viral. I have not found the pus to contain bacteria; rather, it seems to flow at a remarkable rate and antibacterial dyes painted on the lesions are to no avail. The dyes are pushed out in a couple of hours by the fast-flowing pus. Pus streaked out on agar plates was sterile. A few aquarists have had success stopping the course of the disease with tetracyclines; these are wide-spectrum antibiotics. The best guess at this time is that we are dealing with bacteria infecting the nervous system around the head, but their numbers are very small in proportion to the damage they cause. Until the organism is isolated, however, we will not be able to do laboratory determinations of which antibiotics are most effective. It is also possible that a virus begins the damage, and the bacteria are secondary invaders. If this is the case, then we are in trouble, as there are practically no cures for viruses, and there are certainly none for fish viruses at present.

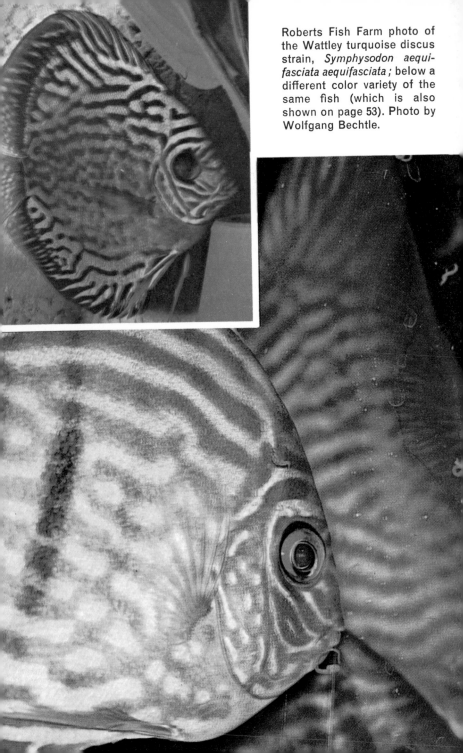

Roberts Fish Farm photo of the Wattley turquoise discus strain, *Symphysodon aequifasciata aequifasciata*; below a different color variety of the same fish (which is also shown on page 53). Photo by Wolfgang Bechtle.

COMMENT OF A COMMERCIAL BREEDER

BY JACK WATTLEY

Discus fanciers are presently having excellent results both in maintaining and in spawning their discus. This is partially due to our present knowledge of the water changes, water temperature, and food that discus require. Also, discus are being shipped into the United States in much greater quantities now that so many more quality fish are available.

Nearly all discus arriving in the States by airplane are packed and shipped from four of the major tropical fish collecting areas of the Amazon Valley. Besides Belem do Para and Manaus, Brazil, many discus arrive from Leticia in Colombia, and from Iquitos, Peru. Generally speaking, most brown discus are brought in to Belem, with both blues and heckels centered around Manaus. The greens are collected on the Putumayo River in northern Peru, and are shipped out of Iquitos and Leticia.

Located in Manaus, Brazil, is the discus king of the Amazon, Senhor H. W. Schwartz, who is known to all as Willi. All of the known color varieties of discus can usually be found at his location. As Dr. Herbert R. Axelrod has said in many of his *T.F.H.* articles, Willi also collects and ships out great quantities of one of the most popular of all tropical fish, the cardinal tetra (*Cheirodon axelrodi*). Another big discus shipper is Rafael Wandurraga, who is located in Leticia. His facilities for holding his fish, plus the quality and conditions of his discus, were the best I have seen in Peru, Colombia, or Brazil.

Most discus are caught with seines in the smaller feeder streams that join the larger rivers. They are easier to obtain during the dry season when the waters are low. This is more or less from September to January. Although the rains begin in earnest in most parts of the Amazon in December, the rivers really don't begin to rise until January or February. During the peak of the dry season, discus can be found in very shallow brooks where the water is very clear in color, and not more than 18 inches deep. These little brooks are fairly fast moving and have a water temperature of about 72 degrees F. The cool water is the result of the brooks winding through the very densest part of the jungle where the sun is never given the chance to warm up the water. Discus found in this type of location were very obviously trapped when the waters began to recede. The ones I encountered were all suffering slightly from fungal invaded abrasions of some sort, and the very cool water did not give the wounds a chance to heal.

Some of the fish exporters along the Amazon have their own collecting crews, while others purchase their discus from local fishermen. A very crucial period in the life of the newly caught discus is from the time it is taken from its jungle stream until it reaches the importer's holding tanks in Florida or New York. During this time the fish is subject to radical pH water changes, temperature changes, overcrowding in dirty containers, and most important a lack of oxygen in the water. Brain damage is the result of oxygen starvation while crowding discus in small containers for too long a time with no water changes, and there is absolutely no cure for such a condition. I have seen many discus in such a state, ready for export to the States, with no hope for their survival. Upon arrival in the hobbyist's aquarium, discus in such a state generally dash about wildly, with no equilibrium. The head may be tilted up towards the surface or down towards the bottom of the tank in this state.

Needless to say, there will be some very basic equipment needed for the discus enthusiast, such as nets, heater-thermostat units, thermometers, medication, syphon hoses, plastic buckets, phosphoric acid (or some other type of acid), etc. The only desirable nets for moving discus are about 10 inches by 7 inches in size, and are made of nylon or soft cotton. Generally discus aren't difficult to catch in a net, if they haven't been unduly frightened beforehand. One of the best investments to make is purchase of a good, reliable thermometer. The average aquarium thermometer probably won't be correct, or if it is at the time of purchase, will usually go bad within a short time. I have recommended to many discus fanciers a ten dollar thermometer that can be found in any photographic supply house. And depending on the make, it will clip on to the side of the aquarium, with a metal stem extending down into the water about six inches. These are extremely accurate and easy to read, and can be quickly moved from tank to tank. Heater-thermostats can be another bug-a-boo to discus keepers. There is no poorer investment than a cheap, poorly made heater. Covers for discus tanks are to be greatly recommended. Discus are great jumpers, especially when nervous. The nervous condition is caused by a high bacteria count in the water, due to excess feeding in most cases. Very satisfactory covers can be homemade of plastic screening and narrow wood frames.

Many jungle discus refuse to eat when finally put in the hobbyist's tank at home. This is due to the fact that they probably have had no food since being caught, and their appetite is deadened. Most of the Amazonian collectors don't bother to feed the new fish, as they are generally shipped out within a week or so. But the fancier can combine several methods to make even the most stubborn discus eat. Assuming the aquarium water is clean and fresh, the temperature can be raised from the usual 82–84° to 90° F. This alone will increase the metabolism of the discus, thus making them more interested in eating. And the water can be made a bit more acid, say down to about 6.0 pH. The addition of another discus, one that has been around for some time and is eating well, will usually induce the new discus to eat when they see it eating. As a last resort, the feeding of live white worms or tubifex worms may do the trick. I don't generally approve of the feeding of either live tubifex or of live white worms, but sometimes it is necessary. If you do have to resort to worms, try white worms first as they are much cleaner than live tubifex.

After your new discus are eating live brine shrimp you can gradually mix some frozen adult brine shrimp with the live and they should take it. The next step is to add a prepared, mixed food to the frozen shrimp, and when they greedily accept that, your feeding problem is past. The conversion from live adult brine shrimp to a frozen, mixed food may take a month or so.

H. Willi Schwartz who owns Acquario Rio Negro in Manaus, Brazil has collected and exported more discus than anyone else in the world. He stores his fishes in dirt pools. These photos show views of his compound outside Manaus.

Some discus crave worms so much that it is nearly impossible to get them on to a prepared food, but it can be done. Sometimes it may be necessary to fast the fish for several days in order for them to become sufficiently hungry to accept a new food, and the withholding of the food for this length of time will not in any way harm the fish.

All successful discus feeding programs are very simple. All of my discus, except fry and very young fish, are fed twice daily. Large adults are fasted one day per week. This fasting for a day gives their intestinal tract a good chance to get thoroughly cleaned out, and the fish always greet their owner the following day with added interest. The morning feeding consists of my prepared mixed food and the late afternoon feeding is of either live adult brine shrimp or frozen brine shrimp. In both of these feedings the fish are fed a goodly amount, so that the stomachs can be seen to bulge a bit. All of this food is to be consumed within a period of several minutes, although the fish continue to pick from the bottom of the bare tank for tiny particles of food for another ten minutes or so. In the feeding of frozen brine shrimp it is of paramount importance that the shrimp be of good color and consistency. If the shrimp is black in color, and if there is the slightest doubt that the shrimp has been previously defrosted, throw it away! Good frozen brine shrimp can be red, brown, or even a grey-green in color, but never black. Try to purchase the largest package of shrimp possible, as there will be less chance of it having been previously defrosted. The tiny packages of shrimp, which are very thin, begin to thaw out in a few minutes if exposed to the air. (I have adhered to my own proved successful feeding program despite the advantages offered by the freeze-dried brine shrimp now widely used.)

The mixed food I use consists of three parts uncooked shrimp (the kind we all eat in shrimp cocktails), and one part uncooked beef heart. The shrimp is peeled, and the heart is thoroughly trimmed, and all of this is then put through a meat grinder and a blender. To five pounds of this mix is added four small packets of unflavored gelatin that has been heated and dissolved in a small amount of water. Aside from the protein value, the gelatin tends to bond the mix together. All of this can then be put in the freezer in small individual packets carefully wrapped. There are many fish food mixes that are more or less similar to this one, and I have used some of them with good results. One can add to a mix such as this one the following with excellent results: grated cheese, skimmed milk solids, flake fish foods, blood meal, and egg yolks.

After baby discus are a week old they can begin to take newly hatched brine shrimp and micro-worms. A micro-worm culture is easy to maintain, and can be purchased from one of several suppliers that advertise in the tropical fish magazines that appear monthly. After two to three weeks of age the young discus can begin to take the mixed food, but only if it is scraped very fine. This is very important, as the young discus can very easily become constipated if the food they eat is too bulky or too hard for them to digest. The young fish should be fed three times daily if possible. An ideal schedule for them would be to feed the mix in the morning, the micro-worms in the afternoon, and the live baby shrimp in the evening. And with all discus, give them a good chance to thoroughly finish their food before turning off lights. Don't overfeed with the baby brine shrimp as this will quickly cause constipation. Until the young discus are about one inch in diameter, it is a good idea to make a daily water change of about one-third, adding fresh-drawn tap water to the tank. This action will help to eliminate problems regarding constipation, as the water changes tend to keep the bowels of young discus open.

We are all fully aware that many successful discus fanciers feed tubifex worms or live mosquito larvae to their fish. But with this type of feeding problems develop sooner or later. Both live tubifex worms and live mosquito larvae are loaded with bacteria and fungus spores, and over the years I've personally found that I've had far less trouble when I restricted the diet to the prepared foods and brine shrimp. Discus do like tubifex worms and mosquito larvae, and they can be brought into breeding condition very quickly by using such foods. But ultimately the fish will develop such ailments as head worms, body ulcers, and white feces for no real "apparent" reason. One "worm" I have found to be excellent, and safe, for all discus is the larvae of a moth that can be found in stale bird seed. Hundreds of these little worms can be cultured in the seed, and they will be completely free of bacteria inasmuch as they eat only the bird seed.

Lake Tefe has always been an airplane stop on the Amazon flying boat. The discus, however, are found far from this site. Photo by Dr. Herbert R. Axelrod.

Another word about feeding—never move a discus, especially a large one, from one tank to another on a full stomach. The new tank will have different bacteria in the water, and the fish is apt to become constipated. Try to anticipate your discus moves and don't feed the fish on that day. As stated previously, the short intestinal tract of the discus will be given a rest on the day of the fasting. While fishing on the Jurua River near the town of Carauari in Brazil, I opened up some large discus that were destined for the frying pan, found absolutely nothing in their intestinal tract or gut, and I am certain that all wild discus go many days without any food at different times of the year. Even discus in home aquariums can go six months or so with no food, though this isn't advocated.

In the jungle streams, discus no doubt eat tiny fresh water shrimp as well as small insect pupae and caterpillars that are found along the submerged banks. One of the local fishermen in the town of Tefe, Brazil, told me the discus eat *lima*, which I found to be algae, but I question that they do eat algae. Some aquarium discus do pick at algae, but it is nothing more than infrequent picking. Many discus fanciers are having good success using bare tanks. Mine are bare, and employ inverted flowerpots

Mueller-Schmida photo of brown discus.

with plastic sword plants extending from the holes of the pots. Spawning discus will readily deposit eggs on the sides of the pots, and there is not the risk of the pots being tipped over, as will often happen with pieces of slate. It is only to add a bit of greenery to the tank that the plastic plants are used. Natural, live plants don't do well in my discus water, with a pH of about 6.3.

Needless to say, the larger the tank the better. As the discus begin to approach adult size, a 50 gallon tank shouldn't house more than five or six fish. My tanks have no sand on the bottom and they all have some sort of a background. A paper background will do well, as the discus generally don't feel secure in a tank with no place to back up to. Glass bottom tanks are easier to keep clean and no doubt have less chance to harbor excessive bacteria than a tank with a slate bottom. Paper should be also put on the bottom (outside) of the tank, if the bottom is glass. A dark bottom background will show up the fish differently than a light colored bottom will. My Turquoise discus show up much more attractively on a darker background, as all discus tend to pale out a bit if the bottom, and the total atmosphere is too light. Plywood tanks that have been epoxied make excellent discus tanks and discus will usually feel secure with the back, the bottom, and the two sides being closed off with wood. Hiding places aren't at all necessary, and too many rocks, plants, or objects will keep many discus on the timid side. Discus also become timid if the light in the room or in the aquarium isn't sufficient. A 50 gallon tank with two or three flowerpots with plastic plants will afford five adult discus all the space necessary, even if there is a bully in the tank.

Discus usually establish a "pecking order" and there is always some chasing, fin nipping, and pushing in an aquarium of healthy full-size fish. This condition isn't serious, even though one discus has clearly been established as the bully of the tank. At times, however, several discus will continually harass the weakest fish in the tank to the point that it will hang off in a corner and won't eat. In such circumstances it is best to remove the weak fish.

Discus do best by themselves, but if other fish are to be kept with them a few *Corydoras*, small tetras, or dwarf cichlids would be satisfactory. Discus kept with angel fish usually become completely intimidated by the more aggressive and swifter-moving angels, and will not get their share of food at feeding time. None of the sharks (*Labeo*), loaches (*Botia*), or barbs are suitable either, as they tend to nip the fins of the discus and to bother them unneccessarily.

Probably the biggest breakthrough in successful discus keeping has been the fact that they do extremely well with frequent water changes. I change about one-fourth of the tank water twice weekly, adding fresh water directly from the tap without aging it. The discus have to be gradually conditioned to this chlorinated water, naturally, but I feel certain that the small amount of chlorine that finds its way into the aquarium is beneficial in that it no doubt kills some harmful bacteria. By the end of several hours the chlorine is dissipated anyway.

My water is kept at a pH of about 6.3. The only big advantage to an acid pH is the fact that bacteria propagate more rapidly in alkaline water. Newly imported discus do need acid water initially, as the typical discus water of the Amazon region is very soft and quite acid, and almost bacteria free. The native fishermen have absolutely no qualms about drinking it. This water is extremely clear, and blackish in color. This is due to the extracts of the leaves, branches, and bark that are in constant contact with the water. This blackish, sterile water looks exactly like coffee or strong tea before adding cream.

Most water as drawn directly from the tap will be quite alkaline, but it can be made acid by the addition of phosphoric acid (or one of several other acids) which can be purchased or ordered from any drug store and are not expensive. I have experimented with discus in very acid water and have found that they do well in water with a pH count as low as 4.5. Your bromothymol blue pH test kit will not register readings that low, so a methyl red testing kit will be necessary to test water on the very acid side. But, as mentioned before, discus do well in water only moderately acid, of about 6.3 to 6.5, and the extremely acid water of 4.5 is not at all necessary.

If one makes frequent water changes, and doesn't foul the water by feeding the discus too much, the type of filtration used isn't of too much importance. If bare tanks are to be employed, with no sand, a very practical, easy to clean filter is of the sponge type. In each of my 50 gallon tanks I use two sponge filters, and these are quickly cleaned about every two to three weeks. Outside power filters are also very efficient, using Dacron, charcoal or carbon, and even peat moss. The peat will tend to keep the water on the acid side. The sponge filters are especially good when one is raising young discus, or any other fry for that matter, as the tiny fish can't be drawn into the filter in any way. And they like to pick at the tiny food particles from the surfaces of the sponge.

Regardless of the source of new discus, never add them to an already established tank without first having isolated the new fish for at least three weeks. Many times discus illnesses and diseases won't show up until the new fish has been in the tank for several weeks. Meanwhile, don't transmit any possible disease by dipping hands or nets, or transfer objects from the new tank to any established tanks. Usually the first sign of something wrong in your discus tank is the darkening of the nine vertical bars that all discus have. A healthy discus that is being harassed by another discus, or one that is temporarily constipated will show the nine bars, but this is generally only a temporary thing. But a sick discus nearly always shows the nine stripes very pronounced all the time, with the stripe running through the head being especially dark. The Negro River discus, *Symphysodon heckel*, however, shows pronounced vertical stripes many times even when healthy. This discus is commonly known as the red heckel or the blue heckel.

If the new discus shows nothing more than a bit of fin fungus upon arrival there is nothing much to worry about. Heat alone will cure this without your having to add any medication. A raise in the water temperature from 83° F. to about 90–92° F. is sufficient. Discus can stand temperatures a bit beyond 100° F. with proper aeration; but, if one is treating for bacterial diseases, this high temperature is useless as the bacteria can also stand the same high temperature.

At times discus that have been tame and calm for months suddenly become jumpy, frightened, and nervous when anyone approaches their tank. In all probability the keeper has unknowingly fed larger quantities of food little by little, until at last the water has acquired an extremely high bacteria count, or worse yet, the discus have begun to harbor an excess of harmful bacteria in the intestinal tract. This condition can be quickly remedied by the immediate cessation of all feeding for several days with adult fish (one day with young fish), and with the addition of one copper sponge per 20 gallons of water. Also, change one-third of the tank water before starting treatment. These sponges, which are used in the home kitchen for scouring pans, can be bought in any supermarket. Be sure to get the ones with no soap added. After three days remove the sponges, drain and replace one half of the water, and begin a more moderate feeding program. If the tank water is very acid, keep a very close watch after the first day and a half to two days; the copper will dissolve much quicker into the acid water than it will into alkaline water, and the fish may show signs of some distress after a day or so in this water. Copper is lethal to fish, so do not add to the dosage and do keep a close watch on the discus. In some stubborn cases it may be necessary to add sulfa drugs to the water if the copper doesn't do the job. It is not necessary to remove the copper before adding the sulfa. Each of the 250 mm tablets contains sulfadiazine, sulfamerazine, and sulfamethazine. Add one tablet for each seven gallons of water, preferably every eight hours for three days.

S. aequifasciata axelrodi.　　　　Mueller-Schmida photo.

Very young discus are especially prone to digestive disorders, and as a preventative I keep one sponge of copper in each 50 gallon tank at all times. The sponge loses its effectiveness when it becomes tarnished, at which time it can no longer inhibit bacterial growth, and at that time it is thrown out and replaced with a new one. And by making frequent water changes, the amount of copper that leaches out into the water is very small. At times such as these, an inexpensive copper test kit comes in handy. Discus can develop white, stringy feces if they are fed an excess of food that is too hard for them to digest, such as bloodworms (*Chironomus*), or *Gammarus* shrimp, or if they eat any brine shrimp or prepared food that has spoiled. This condition can be cured by using the copper/sulfa treatment, along with a big initial water change, and the fasting of the adult discus for several days (baby discus to be fasted one day).

If freshwater live food is fed to discus, it is very possible the fish can become infested by gill flukes (*Gyrodactlus*). The flukes will cause the discus to breath rapidly, but this isn't too serious if detected at an early stage. Add two drops of formaldehyde per gallon of tank water directly to the aquarium once a day for two days. It won't be necessary to make a water change at the end of the treatment, as should be done after any copper treatment, since the formaldehyde will be completely dissipated by that time.

For discus "head worms," body lesions, and general wasting away, which may be a form of *Ichthyphonus hoferi*, success in treatment may be obtained by using 88% phenol. This is also known as carbolic acid. The stock solution is made up of one part carbolic acid to 100 parts of distilled water. The treatment is to last for no more than five days, and the fish are to be observed very closely. At the first sign of any distress, which could be either a very rapid rate of respiration or a darkening of color of the fish, or both, the discus should be immediately removed from the medicated water and placed in another tank. If this distressed condition is to appear it will generally do so after the third or fourth application. For the first day of the treatment add three ounces of stock solution to each 50 gallons of aquarium water. For each of the next three to four days add one ounce of the stock solution to each 50 gallons of water in the tank. Twenty four hours after the final treatment, a water change of about one third can be made.

Another treatment for body lesions and advanced fungus is with the drug Tetracycline. This can be combined with Mycostatin. The combination of the two drugs is called Mysteclin F. One capsule (250 mm) per 25 gallons of water is to be used, once per day for two days. Keep the aquarium completely covered, as the Tetracycline usually makes the fish a bit jumpy. The Tetracycline should not be used in conjunction with any of the sulfa drugs at any time.

Many persons in the United States, the Orient, and in Europe are presently breeding discus. What had been not too many years ago a real feat, is fast becoming a common occurence. Most of the Orientals breeding discus are doing so purely from a commercial standpoint. They use an overpowering technique in obtaining breeding pairs. Many hundreds of large discus are imported and are put into large tanks and allowed to pair off naturally. They are fed a diet mainly of live tubifex worms (which abound in Japan), and are kept in warm, acid water. All of this puts them in breeding condition quickly. But, these breeders also lose huge quantities of the breeders, which I believe would have to be attributed to the feeding of the live worms. Most of the Oriental discus are of the brown variety, although some fairly nice looking blue discus are coming to the local scene from Hong Kong, Bangkok, and Japan.

Many times discus will spawn with absolutely no advance notice to the breeder. I have had pairs of my Turquoise strain show no signs of breeding for the first time until the actual day of the spawning. The breeding tubes of neither the male nor the female were extended to any degree. Suddenly they would chase the rest of the discus away from one end of the aquarium, hurriedly peck and clean a section of a flower pot, and within an hour or so begin to spawn. Most discus spawnings take about an hour to complete. One can be fairly certain of having a pair if the two fish continually keep to themselves and defend one section of the tank, driving off all intruders. And generally several days before the actual spawning takes place, the anal and caudal fins of both fish will take on a much darker appearance (turning a dark grey color, especially in the male). At this time both discus will do little "dances" for the other one. This consists of sidling up to the other mate with head tilted upwards, and softly twitching the tail end of the body toward the other fish. Violent body lashing and fighting, though, have absolutely nothing whatsoever to do with discus pairing off.

After the spawning is completed, the pair will fan and guard the eggs. If the eggs are destined to be eaten by the pair it usually isn't the first day. And many times one of the fish is the model parent, and has to fight off the egg-eating mate. And other times the pair will guard the eggs well and then turn on the fry and devour them. I have found that slamming doors, walking in front of the tanks, turning lights on and off, and similar disturbing actions has absolutely nothing to do with the pair eating their eggs or fry. In fact, I'm beginning to believe that these things might tend to make the pair guard their spawn even more closely than usual. In some pairs of discus the instinct to guard the spawn is greater than in other pairs. But I have had lethargic pairs of fish that continually ate their spawn on the second day suddenly turn into "tigers" upon the introduction of several more discus immediately after the spawning. With the introduction of the new discus to the tank, the breeders vigorously guarded the spawn from the intruders, driving them away from the flower pot where the eggs were laid. In some cases the pair continued to guard the spawn after hatching, at which time a tight-fitting glass partition was placed very close to the spawn. This allowed the remaining discus in the tank to move very close to the parents and fry without being able to eat the fry. In cases such as this, the parents fly into a rage and turn a clay color around the head when the other adult discus hover near the glass partition, and it is at this time that the paternal instinct to guard the "nest" is at its greatest. This method does not work at all times, as some breeders do eat the eggs or fry all the time, but before I was able to raise my Turquoise discus fry away from the parents, it worked for me on many occasions.

Certainly in the jungle streams, discus pairs have to continually guard and defend their spawns from predators of all sorts, and there is nothing more unnatural than a pair of discus in a home aquarium all by themselves, with both sides of the tank covered, and with complete peace and quiet.

Like angel fish, discus will spawn (if the eggs are removed and hatched artificially) every seven days or so when they are in their spawning cycle. If the pair are allowed to successfully rear their own young, the fry will begin to pick and eat from the parents' sides the seventh day after the eggs have been laid. As stated previously, if other discus are in the same tank with the breeders, a tight-fitting glass partition will have to be placed between the pair with fry and the other fish, before the fry become free swimming.

The baby discus will grow quickly while grazing from the sides of the parents. They can usually be removed to their own tank after about eight or nine days of feeding from the parents. Occasionally the parents become belligerent toward one another and it will be advisable to remove one of them and allow the remaining parent to raise the spawn. The remaining parent will usually raise the spawn with no trouble. Such fighting may occur while the pair guard the eggs, and it is best practice to remove one of the two. Two or three days before moving the fry to their own tank, it will be necessary to begin feeding them newly hatched brine shrimp. This can be done very easily by placing the shrimp close to the sides of the parents while the young are feeding, and in some cases the baby discus will immediately take it. If this feeding is done several times a day for two days, the fry will be seen to dart through the water after the shrimp. You will have to observe this rather closely, as the young discus will not venture very far from the parents' sides while looking for the shrimp. Under no circumstances move the fry to another tank until you are certain they are accepting the shrimp.

A five gallon tank is more than sufficient to house the fry after the removal from the parents. In a tank of this size (even with 100 or more fry) they will be able to find their food easily. One small sponge filter will do a good job, and by the second day in this tank the fry will be seen hovering around the sponge and picking food from it. In making the transfer from the breeding tank, use the same water. After a week or so in the small tank the young can be transferred to a much larger tank, as by this time their feeding reflexes will have become much more fixed and they will be able to track down their food in all reaches of the larger tank. After having been in the larger aquarium for a week, the mixed prepared food can be introduced gradually to them. It must be grated very fine, and any that isn't consumed within an hour has to be completely siphoned out of the tank. They may not take this new food at first, but if it is presented to them daily, along with the usual shrimp feedings, they should begin to pick at it within two days, and before long they will like it more than they do the shrimp.

Discus do not spawn the year around; they go off of their spawning cycle for an occasional rest. These resting periods don't last more than six to eight weeks, but there are times when they refuse to get back on a regular spawning cycle. In the Amazon Valley, discus spawn when the waters are very high and the food is most plentiful. At such times, the pH of the water will change. During the dry season, when the streams are very shallow, the water will be extremely acid (5.5 to 6.0). But during the rainy season, when the forests are deluged with almost constant rain, the steadily rising rivers and streams will take on a less acid condition. This is when the discus will spawn. Therefore, if one has a pair of proven breeders that refuse to spawn, it is possible to trigger them to spawn by making larger than average water changes, and at the same time readjusting the pH of the water. If the water was being kept at a pH of about 6.3 readjust it over a period of two days to a reading of about 6.8 to 7.0. If this doesn't trigger the pair to spawn, drop the pH back down again and start over. Assuming the pair to be in good condition, the pH changing, plus the water changes, should have an effect within two weeks. The degree of hardness of the water (DH) isn't of too much importance, as long as the water being used is not extremely hard. Yet it is known that several successful breeders of discus in Los Angeles, California, have bred discus using their very hard local river water. One need not worry about DH as long as it doesn't go too far beyond a reading of 180 ppm (10 DH).

As stated previously, the majority of discus presently being spawned are either of the brown or of the blue variety, with some infrequent spawnings of greens. But no one has had any consistent success with the heckels. They are decidely a more timid, more delicate fish than the rest, and they probably require a bit more care than the other discus do in order to achieve breeding success. If heckels are in the same large tank with other discus, they will usually be observed to group by themselves and to be a bit timid.

CRITIQUE ON MR. WATTLEY'S ARTICLE

by DR. HERBERT R. AXELROD

When I asked Jack Wattley to write an article about his experiences, I did so because he does successfully raise many discusfishes. I didn't expect Jack to submit a scientifically accurate article; neither did I expect to have to write this qualifying critique.

I didn't want to edit Jack's article for fear of changing the meaning of what he wanted to say. But I must point out some of the areas with which I must take active disagreement because it might lead the inexperienced discus breeder to a disaster.

One further note: Jack Wattley does not, as far as I know, keep the baby discus with the parents. He feeds the babies on a "secret formula" by a "secret method." I was disappointed that Jack didn't disclose, to some degree, this fact. I must, therefore take exception with most of his feeding suggestions. The following remarks were those with which I take exception:

"Nearly all discus arriving in the States by airplane are packed and shipped from . . . the Amazon Valley."
This is not true. More than 50% of the young discus imported into the U.S.A. comes from southeast Asia, especially Hong Kong, Bangkok and Singapore.

". . . very cool water did not give the wounds a chance to heal."
While the temperature of the water may have some bearing on the speed with which wounds will heal, the 72° water probably did more to harm the fish's ability to be active, catch food, and avert its enemies than to hinder the wound from healing. Thus the 72° water probably caused the fungused wounds rather than preventing them from healing.

"Brain damage is the result of oxygen starvation while crowding discus in small containers for too long . . ."

I do not believe anyone has ever proven that fishes which have suffered brain damage from lack of oxygen have ever lived; nor has anyone shown that discus suffer brain damage from insufficient oxygen.

"I have recommended to many discus fanciers a ten dollar thermometer that can be found in any photographic supply house."

The same manufacturers of photographic thermometers make aquarium thermometers. If you get an accurately calibrated aquarium thermometer to begin with it will work as well as a ten dollar thermometer. The problem with aquarium thermometers is the calibration (starting temperature) only.

"Discus are great jumpers, especially when nervous. The nervous condition is caused by a high bacteria count in the water."

I don't believe this. Discus probably jump because they are frightened and want to escape from a given situation, or are being poisoned or frozen (or cooked) and must escape their environment. I have never found there to be any correlation between "bacteria count" and "nervous jumping."

"grated cheese" is recommended as an additive to fish foods.

I never found a discus which would eat grated cheese and it would foul a tank much faster than anything else Mr. Wattley recommends.

"Don't overfeed with baby brine shrimp as this will cause constipation."

This is completely contrary to my experience, as well as everybody else with whom I have discussed this problem. Baby brine shrimp are 90-92% water and it's hard to envision this kind of food as being so indigestible as to cause constipation.

"Hundreds of worms can be cultured in bird seed and they will be completely free of bacteria inasmuch as they eat only the bird seed."

This is just not true. The worms will probably have just as

much bacteria in and on them regardless of what they eat (exclusive of laboratory diets and worms raised to be "clean").

"Never move a discus with a full stomach. The new tank will have different bacteria in the water and the fish is apt to become constipated."
While I agree that you shouldn't move discus which have just overeaten, it's not because of the "different" bacteria in the water! I challenge the fact that "different" bacteria cause constipation. The constipation problem that Mr. Wattley finds so frequently in his discus is probably from such poor feeding habits as he recommends.

"Discus in home aquariums can go six months or so without food."
This isn't true. The longest a discus has lived without feeding (having food offered to it) was 97 days and the last ten days it never got off the bottom of the tank!

"Typical discus water of the Amazon region is blackish, sterile water which looks exactly like coffee or strong tea before adding cream."
This is not true. I found discus in every kind of water, from clear and colorless, to muddy brown and coffee black. These kind of statements make me doubt that Jack ever really caught any discus himself.

"The Negro River discus, Symphysodon heckel."
There is no *Symphysodon heckel*. It should be *Symphysodon discus Heckel*.

Mr. Wattley further states that because Japan has plenty of tubifex worms, all Far Eastern discus are fed Japanese tubifex. First of all, Japan doesn't export tubifex. Japan imports tubifex from Taiwan to feed eels. Secondly, Japan doesn't export any discus that I have ever heard of. They get more for discus on the local market than they could get for exporting them. Almost all the discus raised in the Far East come from southeast Asia, namely, Hong Kong, Bangkok and Singapore. Taiwan and Japan do not export discus.

DISSENT ON DISCUS

BY DR. ROBERT W. BURKE

I have read every article available to me on discus fishes, and disagree with much that has been written. In writing this article, I make no claims to being an authority; my purpose is merely to share with others my observations of this beautiful and marvelously adaptable fish. To begin, I shall comment briefly on some of the ideas generally held about these fishes.

They are difficult to keep. Nothing is further from the truth. A healthy discus can take a considerable amount of abuse. I have moved discus from one tank to another, from temperatures of 80° to 90° and from pH 7.8 to 5.8, and returned them to the original setups without any ill effects or apparent concern being shown. I usually make such transfers just before feeding time but that has not always been the situation.

Discus require soft, acid water. Mine not only thrive in water of different quality, but I have bred them in water at pH 7.6 and so hard that salts were caking and falling off the heater.

Discus are inclined toward hunger strikes and are infested with headworms. Here a distinction must be made between wild and tank-bred fishes. With one exception, I have not observed a hunger strike exceeding two weeks among tank-bred discus over eight months old. Again with one exception, none of my tank-bred fishes has become infested with headworms however common the affliction may be among imported fishes.

I have kept discus for something over eight years. Until 1964 I had only browns and a few nearly colorless Peruvian greens, but in that year I bought a pair of "mated Hong Kong blues." These were actually browns and they habitually ate their eggs so I broke up the pair and remated the female. From this beginning and using eight pairs as breeders, I have reared over 2000 discus.

The Amazon river and its tributaries is the home of the discus but they are also found in adjacent streams beyond the borders of Brazil. They are very adaptable fish and inhabit placid lakes and swift-flowing small streams as well as the large, slow-moving

117

rivers. In the wild they are not usually very colorful fishes and the infrequent appearance of any blue coloring would indicate that bluish tints are controlled by recessive genes.

Breeding better blues has been my endeavor for several years. My breeding tanks range in size from 60 to 150 gallons, but I have seen discus spawn in a 30 gallon tank and know of a successful spawning in a 5 gallon aquarium. And on one occasion a pair spawned for me and raised their brood in a community tank.

No hobbyist would approve my breeding procedures yet they prove successful. My water would be considered very poor, and even a powerful filter would fail to clear it completely of color. The pH is about 8 and I reduce it to about 7 for spawning. Gradually the acidity builds up; if the pH drops down around 5.5, I build it up to 6.6 or 6.8 but otherwise give it little attention. I do not change water as frequently as most breeders do although I believe with them that such changes probably encourage spawning. I am informed by an acquaintance who has bred many discus that her fishes cease spawning unless she changes 30% of their water periodically. On the other hand, my most productive pair are Peruvian greens in a tank which has never had any change of water except in the replacement of that which has evaporated. With the others, I have found that a change from one tank to another will often induce spawning.

I have never seen any of the reported jaw-locking preparatory to mating, but I have noted that these fishes sometimes perform *shimmy* dances during the period of a day or two before spawning. Sometimes a pair perform together, often while facing the slate; at other times, one of the fish will suddenly assume an angled attitude and exhibit such quaking. The dorsal and pelvic fins blacken in the posterior section during these performances.

Temperature is important and should never be permitted to fall below 80° or discus will sicken. They fare best at 82–84° and should not be overfed. Moreover, in every instance in my experience, when temperature fell to 78° the fishes with spawn ate their eggs or young, and some of the pairs involved had consistently raised their broods in the past.

It is my belief that discus fishes experience feeding cycles. They will gorge themselves for a month or two and then pick gingerly at their food for weeks. I feed twice daily, but with all fish except small fry I skip one feeding each week. With those that do not come to the front of the tank in some eagerness to eat, I skip a second feeding. If fouled water or intestinal ailment is cause for lack of appetite, it is usually manifested by a hanging string of transparent feces and I have been successful in correcting the condition by feeding live foods and raising the temperature to 90° for three days.

Fry upon emerging from the eggs remain on the hatching slate for a period between two and five days and it has been my observation that those which remain longest have the best prospects for survival. On the twelfth day after hatching, fry are fed newly hatched brine shrimp. When red bellies have been displayed following three feedings, the fry are removed from the breeding tank.

They are placed in tanks that provide them plenty of room to grow and are well fed upon a varied diet. Browns will show a bit of color at four to six weeks but lose it a couple of weeks later; blues begin to color at about five or six months of age and continue coloring until they are past two years old. At seven weeks a discus will have a body about the size of a nickel and is ready for sale, and at ten months some of them at least are mature enough to spawn. Formerly I moved young discus occasionally and discovered that they are rather touchy in the five to seven month age bracket and tended to go on hunger strikes following a move. After the eighth, or no later than the ninth month, they will tolerate being moved without protest.

A tank of at least 12 gallon size is required to rear a discus to adulthood, and one no smaller than 20 gallons must be used for growth of a large fish. Adults are heavily coated with a mucous secretion and considerable amounts of this are passed off into the water. It forms a coating on plants and the glass of the aquarium necessitating a twice monthly cleaning, for which I use paper towels. Because of this, and since light enough for propagation of plants encourages the growth of algae, I use artificial plants exclusively.

As to reported length of life among these fish, I make no comment. But my green Peruvian male is over five years old and shows none of the characteristic signs of aging; he is still fertile and eager to spawn. And so long as he and the others in my breeding string continue to spawn I shall keep hoping to establish a pure strain of blues.

POSTSCRIPT

After this book had been written and designed, I had the opportunity for one last read-through. Two points seem to have been underemphasized for some reason or other and I'd like to clarify them now.

Many discusfishes available on the aquarium market are hybrid crosses between *Symphysodon discus* and *Symphysodon aequifasciata* subspecies. Most discus breeders have been successful in crossing the two species with the exception of the very rare subspecies *Symphysodon aequifasciata aequifasciata*, which probably has only been imported once (alive). There are, therefore, many photographs in magazines and books which show fishes with characteristics intermediate between some of the species and subspecies. The discus species are very easy to distinguish on the basis of color alone and I'd like to present a short description of the four known discusfishes so that everyone can make a determination as to the species he has. Hybrids would, of course, have to be interpolated.

Symphysodon discus: known variously as the "red discus", "Pompadour", "blue discus", "heckel discus" and "royal blue discus" has nine vertical bars evenly divided by three very heavy bars. Thus, bars one, five

and nine are very heavy and always visible while the other bars may not be noticeable at times. Its body is almost completely covered with alternating blue and rust lengthwise streaks.

Symphysodon aequifasciata aequifasciata: known variously as the "green discus" and the "Lake Tefe" discus, is the only discus whose streaks are darker than its body color. The streaks are found on the upper half of the body from the snout to the middle or end of the dorsal fin and on the lower part of the body from the caudal peduncle through the pelvic fins. Its basic body color is green and its lengthwise streaks are dark brown.

Symphysodon aequifasciata haraldi, known variously as the "red discus," "blue discus," the "half blue discus," and the "green discus" has the same basic color pattern as *S.a. aequifasciata* except the body color is reddish brown instead of green and the lengthwise streaks are bright blue instead of dark brown.

Symphysodon axelrodi, the "brown discus," has a basic brown color with blue vertical streaks more or less restricted to the forehead and the anal and dorsal fins.

Anyone can Raise Discus ... Without Their Parents!

BY DR. HERBERT R. AXELROD

In 1968 Carroll Friswold wrote a book with the title *Anyone Can Raise Discus*. In this book Mr. Friswold tells all he knows about discus, and his discussions are very sound and convincing. The book, consisting of nine printed pages, can be purchased for $15 (£6.50) by writing to Carroll Friswold, Altadena Water Gardens, 519 W. Altadena Drive, Altadena, California 91001. The book is worth the money, for its nine pages are filled with more than 30 years of experience.

Basically, Friswold discusses how he raises discus without leaving the young with their parents. While he agrees that in a small percentage of the cases the babies may be left with the parents, they usually are eaten in the majority of cases. His argument, which is believable, suggests that the breeding discus eat their young for reasons other than the health of the young, for those young raised without parents are usually 90% healthy.

Friswold suggests that after the pair spawn they should be left with the eggs for a few hours to be sure that all the eggs have been fertilized. He assumes that the sperm floating or swimming around the eggs will get a chance to fertilize any unfertilized eggs. Inasmuch as the breeding pair are supplied with an almost bare tank, with just a large swordplant or two to make them feel comfortable and safe, they almost always select a piece of slate about 3 inches wide, about a foot long and not more than $\frac{1}{2}$ inch thick. Either red or black slate will do. This slate is then removed with the eggs on it and placed into a clear glass hatching jar of about one gallon capacity.

The hatching solution is water taken from the spawning tank to which acriflavine has been added. Using the Lilly acriflavine, Friswold suggests using .5 tablets. I doubt that he means "$\frac{1}{2}$ tablet." He is probably referring to the weight of the tablet which might be 500 mgs or $\frac{1}{2}$ gram. Using eight of these 500 mg tablets, Friswold makes a master solution by dissolving the tablets in a gallon of water. Assumedly using two tablets in a quart would work just as well. The stock solution is added to the hatching solution at the rate of three tablespoonfuls per gallon of hatching water. Friswold says that the acriflavine inhibits the growth of fungus which would destroy the eggs.

Using a brisk stream of aeration from an air pump and air stone, the water is directed against the eggs in the hatching jar to ensure that there is sufficient circulation around and across the eggs. This aeration serves many purposes besides bringing freshly aerated water to the eggs. It massages the egg and keeps debris from settling on the egg; it removes the products of growth from the egg, and it wrenches loose dead or dying eggs. The air massage acts, assumedly, like the mouthing action of the parents. A further function of the stream of aerated water is the ability of the agitated water to remain at uniform temperature and not be hotter in the immediate area of the heater and cooler farther from the heater. Friswold suggests that the hatching take place at an even temperature of 80° to 82°F. Diffused light is suggested.

The fertile eggs hatch in two to three days and the babies fall out of the shells and conglomerate into wriggling masses at the bottom of the hatching jar. Thus far everything suggests the usual way of hatching and spawning angelfish of the genus *Pterophyllum*.

As quickly as the majority of the spawn has hatched, they should be removed to another type of solution, which might be called a "growing" solution. This growing solution, as suggested by Friswold, is made of half regular water (assumedly tap water) and half distilled water. Friswold's tap water comes from the Colorado River and from deep wells. The pH varies between 7.6 and 8.2 and is quite hard with readings as high as 760 ppm. Friswold doesn't adjust the pH or demineralize the water. He takes it right from the tap. Naturally, the growing solution should be the same temperature as the hatching solution.

The hatchlings are removed to shallow enamel pans which have gently sloping sides and measure $16 \times 11 \times 4\frac{1}{2}$ inches. While the transfer may be made with dips tubes, nets, meat basters or an ordinary siphon, Friswold suggests that you pour the whole gallon hatching jar into the pan, water and all (why not remove as much water as possible since the babies are on the bottom????), and when things have settled down with the babies re-clustered into wriggling masses, siphon off the acriflavine water and replace with growing solution. With Friswold's method there must obviously be some hatching solution left, since you wouldn't siphon off *all* the water and leave the babies high and dry. Friswold isn't clear at all about this point.

Friswold suggests a depth of one inch to the growing solution in the shallow pan, with gentle aeration. He further suggests that methylene blue also works to protect the eggs, but he gives no strength. Probably the amount used isn't important as long as the water is tinted with about 5 drops of 5% methylene blue per gallon (the same strength I use for angelfish of the genus *Pterophyllum*). Friswold stresses the fact that it is important to get the newly hatched babies into clear water as soon as possible. Friswold experiences a 48 hour hatch in water at 82°F. using his hatching methods.

In the trays it takes the babies another week or more before the fry break up their conglomerate existence and become free-swimming individuals. The small fry almost immediately gather at the waterline utilizing the sloping edge of the pan as a support. Friswold suggests that the free-swimming fry be left undisturbed for four hours after they disassociate from the wriggling mass, to be sure that all vestiges of their egg sacs have been utilized.

According to Friswold, the next five days in the lives of the fry are the most critical. He suggests that you follow his instructions closely and carefully, for in nature it is this period of time that the young begin feeding from the sides of their parents. According to Friswold he substitutes egg yolk for parental slime. Not ordinary egg yolk, mind you, but special egg yolk and fed in a very special way.

The egg yolk is the commercial egg yolk which is used by bakers and confectioners . . . and no other will do, according to Friswold.

Ordinary hard-boiled egg is not a good source of egg yolk since it is too dry and crumbly and falls to the bottom of the tray and fouls the water (though he doesn't discuss liquefying the yolk or squeezing it through a fine cloth so it might hang in suspension in the water.) Well, since Friswold undoubtedly is successful, why argue with success? The commercial egg yolk has a tacky, sticky consistency according to Friswold, so that's what you should look for. *Friswold never had success with any other egg yolk!*

Once the babies have been free-swimming for four hours, they are ready for their first meal. Take a small amount of the commercial preparation of egg yolk and, using a finger dipped into the growing solution as a source of water, form the egg yolk into a pancake about $\frac{1}{2}$ inch in diameter and as thin as possible. Press this pancake in a rolling motion onto the side of the pan so that a deposit of egg yolk is left in a long smear just extending above the water line (so it doesn't fall to the bottom). The entire circumference of the pan has to be prepared in this manner with not more than a two-inch gap between smears. The fry are free swimming now and as they congregate on the water line, they almost invariably land onto a mass of food, simulating their landing on one of their parents' backs. Friswold suggests leaving them alone for two hours to enjoy their food in peace. For light, you may use a 25 watt bulb placed about three feet above the pan.

Once the feeding has been accomplished you can judge how good a cook you were by examining the bellies of the fry with a strong magnifying glass. The ones used by engravers, reading lenses, will do very nicely. Under magnification, the bellies should be quite plump. If the fry don't eat they will die. Friswold doesn't suggest that the fry won't eat. He just assumes they will. Obviously, if they don't eat there was something wrong with the pancakes and you need either a different supply of egg yolk, or a better cook! Friswold warns, by the way, that you prepare only enough egg yolk pancakes for one feeding and that once you have handled the egg yolk you never return it to the main stock. He further warns that you stop aeration during feeding.

After feeding for two hours, the baby discus must be removed to another, clean pan with fresh growing solution. Friswold suggests using a 2-ounce Asepto surgical syringe which has a wide enough opening for the sucking in of the babies, and has a clear glass barrel which makes inspection of the fry easier. As each fry is picked up in the syringe, it is transferred to a green plastic dish about four inches in diameter. The almost black babies are easily observed in this green-colored dish and that's why Friswold recommends it. Friswold doesn't say anything about having any water in the dish before you add the babies, but I assume you would have some water already in the dish and I suggest that you use some of the new water which is identical to the growing solution but never before used. When all the fry have been removed from the pan . . . and they hopefully are all fat and plump . . . remove as much water from the green dish as possible, again using the syringe, and then gently dump the fry into the new growing solution in a clean pan.

Friswold says that each feeding and washing sequence takes four hours and he likes four feedings a day. That means you have 16 hours of work each day . . . for five days . . . to rear your batch of discus fry. Since most of us have other things to do in this world besides being nursemaids to baby discus for 16 hours a day, I assume that Friswold wants this to become a family project. He does say that the discus will do well on three feedings a day, for those who don't have the dedication or the time!

After five days of this type of feeding, the fry should be large enough to be weaned onto newly hatched brine shrimp. Friswold has tested weaning times from three days to ten days, and he feels that five days is the best.

The kind of brine shrimp you use is very important. While I assume that Friswold had access only to the San Francisco and the Utah brine shrimp, this doesn't mean that other species aren't available. In Japan, Hong Kong, Singapore and other Far Eastern areas, there is the Chinese brine shrimp egg which is smaller than the San Francisco egg, and assumedly the newly hatched nauplii are also smaller (I haven't measured them). In any case, Friswold advises the use of San Francisco eggs. I recommend that you use the smallest nauplii possible and if you can get some very small nauplii from Roumanian or South African eggs, then by all means use them. Perhaps weaning at 3 days might be possible with a smaller nauplii and save some fairly tedious work.

Setting up your brine shrimp hatch is very important since you want continuous hatches to ensure a constant supply of newly hatched brine shrimp nauplii every morning and evening. Friswold suggests two feedings a day. Of course you have to be careful that you don't pollute the pans with dead brine shrimp lying uneaten at the bottom (or you'll have to change the water twice a day!) So feed the brine shrimp sparingly. I would suggest that you wash the brine shrimp in fresh water before you feed them to remove as much of the salt from them as possible. Feed the shrimp sparingly and give them as much as they will eat. Once the babies stop feeding, you should stop adding shrimp. To be safe, Friswold suggests that you siphon the bottom of the pan after feeding brine shrimp and that you change the water in the pan only once a day.

Examine your baby discus about an hour after you have put in the brine shrimp. Their bellies should be full and show a tinge of red or orange due to the ingested brine shrimp nauplii. While Friswold doesn't tell us what to do if they refuse to eat the brine shrimp, I would suggest that you keep going with the egg yolk. Due to the size or quality of the brine shrimp, it is conceivable that the babies won't take it.

Cleanliness, according to Friswold, is the name of the game. Egg yolk pollutes the water quickly and if you are lax or inefficient in changing the water, the babies will suffer accordingly. So just keep up with the brine shrimp for a few weeks until the babies begin to get the typical discus shape. Then you can begin to treat them like ordinary fish.

First, move them to a tank where they will have more room to swim and grow. The tank needn't be large. I would suggest that you use a ten gallon aquarium half filled with water. As the discus grow, add more water. As the discus are best kept close to their food, I wouldn't put 50 discus babies into a filled ten gallon aquarium right off. Of course the tank should have a heater (it better be submergible or you'll have a problem with a half-filled tank). A gravel bottom with an undergravel filter is suggested.

Food for the growing discus can be almost anything you'd feed angelfish. Friswold recommends finely cut tubifex worms, white worms, micro-worms, screened daphnia or newly hatched mosquito larvae. Assumedly you should keep changing the water as often as possible. Friswold doesn't say anything about this, but my experience is that you can't change the water often enough for discus of any size.

Friswold claims that his strains of discus spawn at ages from 15 to 18 months, though he once had a pair of blue "Tarzoo" which spawned at 9 months of age and had 22 spawnings before they took a rest. His highest record was 407 young from a pair of brown discus, but he averages a hatching of 100-150. At one time Friswold had 2900 babies from 11 pairs.

Friswold suggests ways to get breeding pairs. His suggestions are the usual angelfish methods of putting a dozen of the best babies into a large tank (Friswold uses a 120 gallon aquarium) and letting them pair off naturally. Friswold writes that the last time he tried this method he got four pair out of 11 fish.

Further suggestions in this informative book of Carroll Friswold's include that you keep your discus pairs in 50 gallon tanks, or in groups in larger tanks. He doesn't recommend that discus be kept with other fishes, especially if they are breeding. He warns about overfeeding adult discus as they develop a "bloat" which is incurable. I have never had this experience.

Discus pairs remain as breeding pairs as long as they are together, the same as angelfish of the genus *Pterophyllum*. If one of the pair is lost, they will accept other mates, and crossing different color varieties is not a problem; they act like fishes of the genus *Xiphophorus* where *X. maculatus* readily crosses with *X. helleri* or any of the other members of the same genus.

An interesting note in Friswold's book is that if the breeders are large, the eggs will be large and the babies will generally be large and easier to raise. He claims that the babies of large brown discus are almost as large as baby guppies.

Friswold also warns about the indiscriminate use of acriflavine. When he used water tinted with acriflavine continuously, he found that the babies died at about one inch in diameter without any warning or showing any signs of disease. He assumes they died from an accumulation of poison in the vital organs. The babies should be about one inch in diameter when they are six to seven weeks old.

After the eight pages of fact-filled information, a ninth page, the last page in his wonderful $15 book, describes an alternative method in one paragraph. This method involves growing colonies of rotifers and other aquatic organisms on glass plates and putting them in with the babies for food. Friswold just sort of mentions it in passing. I do the same.

Friswold's methods, with variations, are being used successfully by many breeders. One of the most successful breeders of discus using the Friswold method (with his own secret pancake formula) is Mack Galbreath, who produced and developed the beautiful blue variety known in the trade as "Mack's powder blue discus." Mack is a very capable breeder and he has a hatchery in Fresno, California known as "Mack's Tropical Fish and Hatchery." His fish are sold through World Wide Aquarium Traders, Inc., 4074 Lincoln Blvd, Venice, California 90291. World Wide specializes in discus, I am told.

One word of warning. Early indications tend to confirm that discus raised artificially have trouble raising their own young in a normal manner. Some authorities claim that babies raised on egg yolk instead of parental slime do not develop their own slime coat which would enable them to feed their own fry.